modern lawn care

modern lawn care

the complete guide to a happy & healthy lawn

David Hedges-Gower

the UK's Leading Lawn Specialist

www.modernlawncare.com

The Gables, Lower Chilworth Farm, Milton Common
Thame, Oxfordshire OX9 2JS

Edited by Rupert Waddington

Design and typesetting by Ned Hoste

Proofreading by Nicky Tudor

Photography: See acknowledgements

Printed and bound by CPI Group (UK) Ltd, Croydon, CR0 4YY

acknowledgements

My thanks for this book could almost be a book in itself. But mostly they go to:

My boy Harvey - I wish he was here to celebrate it with me, but he sadly passed away a couple of years ago. He spent many days with me in my office patiently listening to me talk about 'lawns this' and 'lawns that'. Never a day goes by without my missing him.

My beautiful wife Kate and my wonderful daughter Tara, who, also, have spent many years listening to my tales of grasses and the battles we face as outdoor people.

My mother and late father who made me what I am today.

Both Rupert and Ned for guiding me through this process, without which I would be merely sitting in my office with a huge pile of paper.

Phil O'Hagan for also helping me through the minefield of information that my small brain often struggled to process.

Maria at Shickpics and the STRI (Sports Turf Research Institute) for helping me with many of my pictures.

Richard Sheppard and David Smart for spending countless hours reading each chapter.

Throughout this whole process, I have come to learn that talk is in fact easy and making it mean something is far more complex. The book is a very simplified version of what it could be but hopefully you can take what you can from each section and come up with your own perfect lawn.

Thanks to all....

contents

why this book is needed NOW

Science has changed...

The climate has changed...

Lawn care has changed...

But the British lawn remains a national institution!

Nowhere else in the world does something so simple give so much pleasure. However, if you're one of the many hundreds of people who struggle to maintain your piece of turf in tip-top condition, you may not agree! Yes, when it looks good there's nothing to touch a lawn - the lush carpet of the formal gardens, the immaculate stripes of the croquet lawn, the billiard table finish of the putting green. But these are the exceptions, each meticulously tended by the country's finest turf professionals.

What about real-life, everyday lawns - our lawns, the type that must withstand children and pets, droughts and floods, moles and squirrels? How can they give us the same pleasure when they're so hard to maintain? Is it any surprise that many receive only the very basic attention?

Well, this book is about to change all that.

You see, in recent decades we've seen an explosion of interest in gardening, driven especially by horticultural media personalities, experts in everything from roses to recycling. But the poor old lawn wasn't invited to the party. It's no surprise, therefore, that in the absence of expert help, many gardeners were won over by alternative design ideas such as decking, hard landscaping - and even fake grass! This book, written by our most forward-thinking lawn expert, will put the lawn back where it belongs - at the centre of our gardening activities.

David Hedges-Gower is a man who loves lawns - not just 'perfect' specimens but *any* lawn that is designed and maintained *to do the job it needs to do*, from play areas to croquet lawns, immaculate front lawns to golf greens. And with his experience he knows that with the right information and support, a lawn needn't be a bother; it needn't be yet another patch of land dug up to be replaced by easy-maintenance paving or as an excuse for a swimming pool! Your lawn can be something you truly love and enjoy nurturing through the year. And it can be even more than that. Did you know, for example, that the humble garden lawn:

- Filters and absorbs rainfall

- Captures far more CO_2 than your powered mower produces

- Traps much of the dust and debris that falls on our gardens

- Gives us a relaxing environment which reduces stress

- Acts as a sound buffer in noisy locations

- Helps to keep the garden much cooler in summer

- Enhances the look and value of our properties?

So, you should now feel motivated to read on and discover the rewards of good lawn maintenance. When you experience this book's wisdom and easy-to-use advice, then you will rejoice that at last the UK's Lawn Expert has been invited to the party. Happy gardening!

introduction

The 'perfect' lawn is simply the lawn that's perfect for you and for what you need from it.

A uniformly green, meticulously cut and vibrantly healthy area of lawn looks superb - but achieving and maintaining this is a full-time job! Little wonder then that many people look for alternatives - from crazy paving to bark chippings, play areas to patios - anything other than the energy-draining and ultimately disappointing area of grass that is failing to thrive. However, it doesn't have to be this way...

... a healthy lawn does not have to exhaust you (or indeed the planet). The 'perfect' lawn is NOT the type you see at garden shows or fenced off in pristine country houses; nor is it the immaculate golf green, the billiard-table-smooth croquet lawn or Wimbledon's striped Centre Court at the start of the tournament. No, the 'perfect' lawn is simply the one that's *perfect for you* and for what you need from it. All it takes is an informed and realistic approach to your lawn care.

So, the aim of this book is to help you devise a *practical and manageable year-round programme* to maintain exactly the type of lawn you want. And it does this by presenting the most comprehensive expert advice available in a format that suits both the perfectionist and the reluctant gardener alike. Whatever your goals, you will find the information you need in four main sections:

Your lawn in 3-D: your lawn isn't just grass! This section breaks new ground by giving you a fully three-dimensional understanding of your lawn's triple-layer structure - grass, thatch *and* soil - and explains how each one interacts with and depends on the other two.

1. **Techniques**: if you can master each of the basic techniques - or know when it's best to hire professional help - you will be in complete control of your lawn care programme.

2. **Problems**: understanding the challenges your lawn faces, both natural and man-made, will help you to select the best remedy and maintain a well-balanced lawn environment.

3. **Your 12-month Lawn Care Programme**: working in seasons, I help you
    build up an annual lawn care programme for your 'perfect' lawn, helping
    you find your own balance between professional practice and what is
    practical and realistic for you and your garden.

I hope you enjoy reading this book and find it a useful reference for many years
to come. Here's to your very own 'perfect' lawn!

David Hedges-Gower

a brief history of the lawn

Although the lawn seems archetypally English, the original word - 'Laun' or 'Launde' - is in fact Welsh. And by the time lawns as we know them - closely-cut and carefully-cultivated areas of grass - first appeared in the 17th century, the 'Launde' had already been around for hundreds of years but under a different guise.

Grassy areas performed important practical roles in medieval rural life. Outside your modest dwelling you would keep sheep and other animals - and thanks to their grazing habit, the naturally growing mixture of natural grasses, wild flowers and weeds took on the appearance of a very rough lawn. Meanwhile, up the hill at the larger properties and the fortified castles, grass was considered preferable to trees and woodland as it kept the sightline clear for spotting hostile visitors.

However in the 1500s Renaissance France began to see cultivated green areas as aesthetic rather than purely functional items in their landscapes. If you inspected closely, you would see that they often used either chamomile or thyme, both low and close-growing plants with the added benefit of a pleasant fragrance. By the 1600s, the wealthy landowners began to cultivate grasses to achieve an even more impressive finish. And, equipped only with simple hand tools, armies of gardeners were required to maintain these extremely visible status symbols.

By the time England at large was acquiring the lawn habit, our 19th century industrialists rose to the new challenge of inventing more convenient ways to maintain our lawns. Edward Budding is credited with designing the very first lawn mowing machine in 1827, and the first two examples were put into use in 1830, one going to Regent's Park Zoological Gardens, the other being used in the colleges of Oxford. Made from wrought iron, his machines were very heavy and of course relied entirely on manpower. However, with its rear roller driving a gear which in turn drove the cylinder reel onto a bed knife, his basic design is still in use today!

Following World War 2, the English love affair with their lawns really took off, and today the lawn is a much more affordable garden option than ever before. Technology and science have given us everything we need to grow, feed, weed and cut our grass. Well, nearly everything. Even in the 21st century, lawn care is still a hands-on pastime, but one which gives many thousands of people a focus for their gardening and a pride in their gardens.

your lawn in 3-D

How do you judge a lawn's health? Most people go by what they can see – the colour and thickness of the grass. But to take lawn care seriously, we need to know what's going on underneath as well.

There are *three* dimensions to a lawn and hence to lawn care – the grass, the thatch and the soil. In this section I go into this in considerable detail and I know you may be tempted to skip to 'Techniques' or 'Problems', but take a few minutes to continue reading. This will make the rest of the book much easier to follow and will contribute to your lawn care programme and the fantastic lawn you will soon be looking at.

So, this section examines how the three layers of the structure work and how they interact – how the grass can be starved by excessive thatch, how insufficient thatch can lead to dry soil, and how poor microbial activity in the soil can affect both thatch and grass. And for anyone who is trying to minimise their use of chemicals and fertilisers, the really exciting truth is that good management of the triple-layer structure can help you do this. You can achieve a healthy lawn in perfect eco-balance.

Grass

Thatch

Soil

Grass [n] any monocotyledonous plant of the family *Poaceae* (formely *Gramineae*), having jointed stems sheathed by long, narrow leaves, flowers in spikes, and seed-like fruits.
(Collins English Dictionary 2011)

Knowing which grass species are thriving in *your* lawn will give you a better understanding of the appropriate management technique. However, you don't need to become an expert horticulturalist! Unless you have a newly seeded or turfed lawn, it will be almost impossible to identify exactly which specific types of fescues, bents, ryegrasses (also known as turftypes) and other varieties you have, and in what proportions - but for the average domestic lawn, this doesn't matter. What is important is to find out the approximate *proportions* of the main types

which are clearly thriving in your lawn environment, and to work *with* these rather than striving for the dubious benefit of controlling exactly which grasses are in *your* lawn.

In most lawns you will find some or all of three dominant families of native UK grass - bents, fescues and ryegrasses. Any lawn established before c.1980 will probably have both bents and fescues (as well as many other species in smaller quantities). Lawns and new turf laid since then usually contain some dwarf ryegrass (turftypes) as well (you can read more about ryegrasses below). Some grass varieties grow as very small individual plants; others develop lateral networks of off-shoots which spread very enthusiastically (see Bentgrasses, p30). And of course they all grow at different rates.

You will also have a few weeds! And some people welcome these seasonal additions - plants like clover which attracts bees, daisies and buttercups to keep young children amused, and dandelions for the pet rabbit. But if they are seen as *unwelcome* plants (including grasses) blowing in from neighbouring land to invade your lawn, they need to be tackled as weeds.

To summarise: our grass lawn is not the carefully controlled monoculture that we may think it is. And the plant composition is constantly changing too thanks to the natural cycle of flowering weeds, the condition of the thatch layer and the soil and the effects of the changing weather. So let's look more closely at the grass varieties you probably have in your lawn.

the main grass families

FESCUE (*festuca*)

There are many types and cultivars of fescue, each with slightly different characteristics, but they all conform to the following general description.

Fescues are dominant UK grasses - they love growing in all kinds of lawns! While not the greenest of grasses in appearance, fescues play a very useful role in binding together the turf to give a good density. This does mean, however, that if left unmanaged they can crowd out other varieties in the lawn.

Appearance: fescues have a very fine, almost wire-like leaf blade. The three most common types are Slender Creeping Red, Chewings, and Strong Creeping Red. Almost all lawn fescues grow as individual, tufted plants (and some species are used in their fullness as border specimen plants). Exceptions to this include the Creeping Red Fescue which produces slim, horizontal rhizomes enabling beneficial sideways spread.

How they grow: fescues are generally very strong plants and, with their tufted growth, they can give good shade protection to help root systems cope better with drought and heat. Some species, like the Creeping Red, also recover particularly well from cutting due to their rhizome production and shoot density. The downside of the family's strength is the necessity to keep it under control using surface scarification as well as hollow tine aeration and even an occasional top dressing.

Preferred conditions: the beauty of fescues is that they grow in most lawns! They have a preference for a pH of between 5.5 and 7, but will still grow in other soil pHs. They are very good shade-tolerant grasses and, being well suited for short (cylinder) mowing, are ideal for use in croquet lawns and bowling greens.

Management: fescues can be prone to red-thread disease. Good lawn maintenance, including aeration and scarification, should help keep it at bay. In a controlled environment they can survive close mowing, but in a domestic lawn it is best to stick to the cutting heights recommended on page 81.

Ideal use: fescues grow extremely well in the UK and make an excellent general mixture grass. If you don't have them, you should consider adding them for the robustness and turf-density benefits. And if you do already have them in your mix, just remember to use your general lawn maintenance to keep them under control.

The wiry blades of fescues

BENTGRASSES (*agrostis capillaris* or *castenalla*)

Bentgrasses (or 'bents') are another group of grasses native to the UK. Bents are most commonly used on fine turf areas such as golf, croquet and bowling lawns. In the garden, however, they are generally used as 'space-fillers' when repairing or improving areas of the lawn.

Appearance: often referred to as creepers due to their lateral growth habit (see below), bents are tufted grasses with finely-ribbed short leaves.

How they grow: as with fescues, the tuft above ground is supported by its own root system down below. However, some of the plants or tufts are also connected by stolons and rhizomes - horizontal shoots above and below ground - by which the plant can spread sideways and grow new roots and stems. Look closely at any lawn and you will probably spot some stolons 'creeping' across the surface.

Preferred conditions: bents can live in most lawn-types, although they prefer a pH between 5.5 and 7.

Management: bents can cause excess thatch so regular scarification is important. Fortunately, scarifying also reinvigorates the grass growth, leading to more leaf blades. So in one hit you can control its thatch production and thicken up the grass - entirely naturally.

Ideal use: domestic lawns benefit from this space-filling family of grasses; they just need careful control to prevent them from taking over. New seed mixes will typically include bents but sometimes as only 5% of the complete mix. Well-managed, these grasses can really work well for your lawn.

You can see the blue-grey bentgrass growing in the middle of this patch

DWARF RYEGRASS / TURFTYPE
(*lolium perenne*)

Much criticised in the past (see 'Isn't ryegrass bad?' below), dwarf ryegrasses are fast earning their rightful respectability. Grass breeding programmes are continually improving their useful qualities - fast germination, wear-and-tear resistance and a deep green sward - to rival those of our native bents and fescues. They have even been used recently on golf greens. On the downside, their fast growth can be a shortcoming in an established lawn and they are not known for their density. They do, however, have a definite place in the domestic lawn of today and tomorrow.

Appearance: Ryegrasses are tufted plants. The leaf blades are smooth and have small 'ears' at their base.

How they grow: quick to germinate, dwarf ryegrasses also grow much faster than bents and fescues. However their lateral spread is nowhere near as good as other grass species and individual plants are not especially dense (although continual improvements are gradually breeding this in). They are not prolific thatch producers either (which is both good and bad - see Thatch, p40).

Preferred conditions: ideally preferring a pH range between 6 and 7, dwarf ryegrasses do love fertile ground. They can survive however with a much lower NPK (nitrogen, phosphorous and potassium) level while still maintaining a good green colour.

Management: anything seemingly as good and new as dwarf ryegrasses must come with a catch - and they do! Faster growth means more frequent mowing (and blade sharpening). It does however prefer a higher cut than other species, and this will maintain a thicker-looking sward as well. Also, it is not as tolerant of drought as natural species.

Ideal use: dwarf ryegrass is good for all areas especially high-traffic zones. Being quick to establish, ryes form a high percentage of the mix in many newly-turfed lawns and they can be as good as any other species for shady spots.

OTHER TYPES YOU MAY FIND

Smooth-stalked meadow grass (*poa pratensis*): often seen as a blue colour in lawns, this plant can be tricky to germinate but provides good quality grass and spreads laterally via rhizomes.

Annual meadow grass (*poa annua*): Britain's most prolific and common grass, Poa Annua occurs naturally, spreading via millions of seeds when it flowers and is hence found in most lawns (although regarded as an unwelcome weed particularly in top luxury lawns).

Yorkshire fog (*holcus lanatus*): often seen as another weed grass, this plant has become more prevalent in recent years, possibly due to the changing climate. It exudes a toxin which kills most other grasses, hence the prevalent clumping nature of this species.

Smooth Stalked Meadow Grass

A central clump of coarse Yorkshire Fog

"Isn't ryegrass bad?"

It's true that in the past, ryegrass as a species had a bad reputation amongst gardeners. It was an *agricultural* grass with fat and ugly leaves, ideal for grazing but totally unsuited to a cultivated lawn. However, once grass breeders had established a dwarf variety, the Turf Growers' Association (TGA) adopted this as part of its strategy to create an industry standard for turf sold in the UK.

But why did they choose ryegrass?

Well, it is very tough, hard-wearing and has a deep and dark green colour - just what people want from a domestic lawn! The problem is that when used by itself it leads to bare patches in the lawn as it doesn't spread sideways like bents and fescues. And when used in a blend of species it grows vertically much more quickly than other grasses, leading to irregular lawn lengths.

The dark green of the ryegrass sample stands out clearly

Very healthy ryegrass

discussion

Q: Is it easy to change the mixture of species in an established lawn?

The simple answer is 'no' but the best answer is another question - *why would you want to*? Whilst you may have some species over-dominating the sward and needing some control, whatever is growing there clearly enjoys the habitat and climate in your particular garden. You will also have local, self-seeding wild grasses which will be almost impossible to banish, and of course the pH of your soil is extremely difficult to adjust effectively or for a long period.

Q: Is there a 'perfect' blend of grass species?

For a domestic lawn I would answer 'no' as the 'perfect' blend is what best suits your own garden and soil. Learn how to work with these, and you will end up with a good lawn.

Q: How can I identify which grasses I have?

For the mainstream species it's fairly simple to refer to the pictures above and to examine whether your plants are independent or joined by stolons. If you have a new lawn, ask the turf company that supplied it what % mix is meant to be there. You can then see which amongst these are the dominant species in your lawn.

Q: Can I overseed a ryegrass-dominant sward with fescue seed?

If you have new turf, you probably have a high % of ryegrass. A ryegrass sward is quite open in nature, so over-seeding with a fescue grass can be a great way to fill in your lawn.

Q: Can I overseed a fescue-dominant sward with ryegrass seed?

Yes, however you must realise that seeding into this type of sward needs a little more work. Compared to the open space in a ryegrass sward, a fescue sward is much harder for new seed to penetrate. You may have to prepare a seed bed by scarifying quite heavily and possibly applying a top dressing as well.

Q: ... and what about overseeding with bents?

No, this is only recommended for very fine turf lawns.

discussion

Q: Can I remove certain grass species, especially if I am maintaining a high-quality lawn?

It is possible to use specific chemicals to remove ryegrass but it must be done by a specialist.

Q: What can I do to remove unwanted 'clumps' of weed grass?

There are two alternatives - dig them out or kill them with glyphosate-based chemicals*. The aim is to remove them and then replace with either new turf or a suitable seed mixture. There is more information in the chapter on Weed Control, p144.

Q: I have a flowering grass in all the weak areas of my lawn. What is it?

This is annual meadow grass and is the most common grass in the world. However, it is considered to be a weed grass as it can die off at the end of its cycle, leaving bare areas in your lawn. It is an opportunistic, self-seeding grass and is not mass-produced for the domestic market due to very shallow root development and being vulnerable to extreme conditions. Most people will have some annual meadow grass in their lawn and, as there are no chemical controls, it's best to learn to live with it. Just keep it under control by mowing regularly and removing any clippings if it's had a chance to flower.

Annual Meadow Grass

Q: I've heard some mixes contain 'microclover'. What is this, and should I use it?

Microclover, as the name suggests, is a miniature form of the common White Clover. Traditionally, clover has sometimes been regarded as unwelcome in lawns; the leaves are too big and stand out, making the surface uneven. However, clover is also a nitrogen-catching plant which helps retain a healthy green in the lawn during periods of drought as well as sustaining nutrition levels for longer.

Now, microclover does all this but without sticking out awkwardly. It is tiny enough to blend easily into the grass, while filling it out and keeping it healthy. So, unless you object to almost indiscernible but differently-shaped leaves nestling in your lawn, I wouldn't be too worried about using a mix containing this little friend.

Q: Can I add flowering seasonal 'weeds' to my lawn - and will this damage the balance of grasses?

This is certainly possible and can be a great alternative to a conventional green lawn. Flowering weeds will often benefit in the same way and from the same interventions as your grasses, enjoying the healthy living conditions you are maintaining. Just be aware of any restrictions that their flowering periods may place on your aerating and scarifying schedule.

Always follow chemical instructions on the label, or call in a professional who is qualified in pesticide applications

Grass

Thatch

Soil

Lying beneath the green leaf-blades on the surface is a natural accumulation of dead grass plants, stems and shoots, grass clippings, moss and weeds. This is what we call 'thatch'. Over time, it is broken down by microbial action but it occurs unevenly, with stem nodes, crown and roots taking longer to decompose than the leaf blades. When the organic material builds up faster than it breaks down, the result is an increase in thatch.

What is the purpose of thatch?

Thatch is nature's insulation, acting as a cooling canopy over the ground in hot weather and helping retain soil warmth when it's cold. Thatch is also a necessary protective layer without which the ground becomes muddy in the wet or is baked dry under a hot sun. This layer also fills space which otherwise is soon invaded by weeds and moss. A healthy layer of thatch also provides a softer surface for children to play on safely.

Is thatch a problem?

The answer is that it can be *if we don't manage it properly*. If you focus only on the green parts of the lawn that you can see you will soon have too much thatch. As a result the grass will starve while moss and other species take over. Strip the thatch away completely, however, and you leave vital parts of the entire lawn structure unprotected. Little wonder then that mismanaged thatch control is one of the biggest causes of poor lawns.

The **good news** is that the staple parts of your annual lawn programme all help to control the thatch, if done properly. But understanding why and how these interventions work is really important if you want a successful program, so read on!

How does thatch occur naturally?

What we do as gardeners - taming and controlling nature's grass plants - can exacerbate the thatch problem. However, even without our intervention, the plants themselves quite happily add to the accumulated layer of decaying debris. Let's see how this happens.

- **Bent grasses** grow via stolons or runners which, because these grow above the surface, can add to the top layer of the thatch. They look like extensive stretches of dead material if left unattended. Both healthy and poorly growing bents can also produce lots of dead stems, adding to the thatch layer.

- **Fescues** grow via rhizomes just below the surface, giving the spongy feel you sometimes get when walking across the grass. On the surface itself, however, fescues are busy producing multiple leaf blades per plant. As these die off, they add to the surface and sub-surface thatch material.

- **Rye grass** (also known as turftype) is nowadays found mostly (in dwarf variety) in newly turfed lawns and seed mixes. Unlike bents and fescues, it makes hardly any thatch at all but as we do need a controlled layer of thatch, using just rye grass by itself can be a problem! With its open texture and just a few leaf-blades per plant, the lawn soon becomes muddy in the wet. This is why it should only be used by itself in carefully controlled areas such as tennis courts and cricket wickets.

How do we exacerbate the problem?

As gardeners we must *share* the blame for our thatch problems - and ironically it is often the work we're doing to care for the lawns that adds to the thatch dilemma!

Mowing: without being mown, lawns would convert back into meadows. But this simple and vital part of lawn care leads to problems. Cutting the grass is like cutting the top of a hedge; it simply encourages *sideways* growth, leading to thicker and denser growth - too much grass and too much resulting thatch.

Water and irrigation: you may have invested in an expensive pop-up irrigation system, or perhaps you rely instead on nature's rainfall, an unreliable average of between 100 and 200 days each year. Either way, it is hard to have precise control over the watering and the simple equation is that more water leads to more thatch. So, should we be hoping for drier summers? Well, yes and no. Whilst some grass plants will turn brown in dry weather to preserve themselves, others will die off, *adding* to the organic material that makes up the thatch. All that we can do is observe the rainfall and monitor the results in and beneath the canopy.

Fertilising: one result of our 'tampering' with nature to create the garden lawn is that each time we cut our lawn, we're removing the newest green parts; this actually reduces the plant's capacity to store food and water (roughly 70% is stored in the newest leaf-blades). Little surprise then that most of us resort to feeding to keep the healthy green colour which we value so much. But of course, more nutrition leads to more plant growth which means more mowing - which in turn leads to more thatch.

Choice of plant: fescues and bents are our preferred grasses, and why not, being native to the UK? They are comfortable in our climate and, after centuries of cultivating lawns, we're used to them! But they also contribute to the thatch problem, as explained earlier, and the reasons for this are important to remember when deciding to add plants to your lawn. For example, you can use bents as your 'gap fillers', happily creeping over any voids. They are good grasses but, with their multiple leaf-blade production, they are real thatch culprits too. So we need to be aware of the mix of plants we have in our lawns, and consider adjusting this if necessary.

Soil pH levels: We saw earlier that thatch develops when the micro-organic breakdown of the dead plant material lags behind its accumulation. Another influence on this is the pH level of your soil. If it is too acidic, below a pH of 6.0, micro-organism activity is slightly inhibited and thus the thatch is able to increase (see Soil, p52).

How much is too much?

A simple rule of thumb is to have a thatch layer measuring a quarter to a half of an inch at the start of the year (you can find out how to measure it below). But of course, every lawn is different and we all want different things from them, so a more practical way of assessing 'too much' is to be able to identify the symptoms that tell us there is a problem.

How do we measure our thatch?

A simple visual check of your thatch should be a routine part of your program. The best time to do it is just before you begin a new year's programme of work, as what you find out may influence that programme!

You only need to extract a small piece of turf and you can do this using a variety of tools (here, a soil sampling probe).

Symptoms to look out for:

Mowing: when the surface becomes too spongy and uneven (see photo opposite), you might notice that mowing seems harder than usual. This is because the lawn is getting clogged up with excess thatch and the moss which often comes with it.

Water drainage and retention: thatch absorbs water like a sponge, playing havoc with the lawn's natural drainage by preventing water from penetrating the profile. As a result, the thirsty roots go looking for water by travelling upwards. The resulting sickly or dying grass is easily visible. However, many traditional UK lawns contain the native bentgrasses which spread *sideways* across the surface, sending new roots downwards as they go. On an unscarified lawn, these roots may struggle to reach the soil beneath the thatch. In wet conditions this is not a problem but as soon as the thatch dries out, which it will do eventually, the tiny root systems begin to die.

Nutrition: needing to increase feeding is a clear sign of a thatch problem. Acting as a barrier preventing fertiliser nutrients from reaching the soil, thatch starves the plants of the nutrients they need. So, if you are fertilising your lawn and not seeing the desired result, you may be tempted to fertilise and water some more - but this can encourage even more thatch to develop.

Colour loss: along with other signs of poor health (including one species of grass clearly outperforming another), loss of colour is a clear indication that the plants are not happy in their thatch-dominated environment.

Pests: thatch is favoured by all kinds of insects and their larvae. We need insects living in the grass as part of the natural environmental balance, but an increase in leatherjackets and chafer grubs can sometimes indicate a thatch problem.

What's the solution?

Below are the main ways to control your thatch - you can find more information on each in the Techniques section of the book.

Scarification: you may be used to scarification as a moss-prevention method. However, it can be just as good for controlling thatch but the technique differs slightly. I explain moss-prevention under 'If it's really bad' (p103) but to use it for thatch control, refer to 'Maintenance Scarification' (p98).

Aeration: Aeration will help you prevent excessive thatch by improving the environment for microbial breakdown. All types of bacteria are active in your soils and any type of aeration will get them working harder, but the most effective type is hollow-tine aeration (p70) - removing small plugs which simultaneously removes lumps of thatch, particularly 'sub-surface thatch'.

Top dressing: Discussed on page 128, top dressing of sand, soil or loam will penetrate the thatch layer and help break it down at a quicker rate as well as encouraging more bacterial activity too.

discussion

Q: How much thatch should I remove when scarifying?

This is a good question and is where gardeners often trip up. Many people try to remove all the excess thatch in one go and often don't leave enough grass to fill back in. Sometimes hitting it as hard as possible is necessary BUT usually it is better to think in terms of maintenance, not one-off problem-sorting - little and often can be an effective technique.

Q: What should I do with debris?

After scarifying you're often left with mountains of material and wonder what to do with it. The best tip is to try and incorporate it with your normal compost over time. And of course, any moss you gather can be great for natural hanging baskets and even nesting for wildlife.

Q: Will I ever get rid of all the thatch?

The simple answer is NO, and for a good reason! You need some thatch in your lawn and thatch production occurs pretty well every day. The answer is to be in control of it.

Dig out an inspection sample carefully so that you can slip it back into place

Q: Does thatch affect my mowing?

Yes, of course. When you have excess thatch and you walk across the lawn, you can feel your feet sinking into the turf. Well, if the same thing happens to your mower's wheels, the cutting deck of the mower also drops closer to the grass which reduces the effective cutting height. If you find you are having to raise the height more than usual to avoid scalping the grass, thatch may be the reason!

Q: When should I do thatch control?

This depends on your individual lawn - refer to the sections on scarification (p98), aeration (p64) and then work it into your lawn programme (p204).

Q: What can I do to reduce thatch production?

As this chapter explains, you can do several things in collaboration - but they're all routine parts of your annual programme so you should be doing them anyway! Keep a simple, balanced feed programme and understand that overfeeding is a problem. Improve drainage and only irrigate when necessary (we already get many days of natural irrigation!). Top dressing can help by diluting the thatch and also increasing microbial activity (as does aeration). Soil pH is difficult to adjust and I would suggest calling in someone who knows what they're doing (such as a Lawn Care company).

Grass

Thatch

Soil

Books on lawns tend to pay only lip service to the subject of soil. In a way, I can understand this - it's the one part you don't see and the one part that is very difficult to change once your lawn is established. But it is still an absolutely vital part of the triple-layer lawn structure - most grasses simply wouldn't survive without it! Moreover, I think any gardener would be curious to know more about this hidden subterranean world which teems with life, a bustling part of the lawn's micro-environment. And of course there is something you can and should be doing regularly to maintain healthy soil - aeration (p64). What follows will explain why.

Hidden assets - what's *in* your soil?

As gardeners we pay careful attention to the soil in our flower and vegetable beds - but not the soil beneath our grass. When cultivating plants, we hoe, rake, feed and nurture the soil, but in lawn care we just tend to grumble about poor soil that's heavy in clay, compacted or perhaps too free-draining. After all, the aim of any lawn is to carpet the ground and if the grass grows a little bare and soil becomes visible, we do whatever we can to cover it up again. But just look at what's going on down there:

- The soil beneath an acre of lawn can hold about five tons of living organisms; and

- Just one gram of soil may contain up to 5,000 different species of micro-organisms!

Just as the microscopic plankton feed the giants of the oceans, so the soil is bursting with living things which are essential to the natural environmental

balance in the lawn. Soil is alive. Yes, there are the pests which can damage the lawn - leatherjackets, chafer grubs and moles - but also tiny creatures which make a huge contribution by recycling and breaking down organic material.

- It's said that a teaspoon of soil can contain at least a billion individual organisms.

So, even if we do everything we can to hide it, we can still appreciate soil's complexity and its contribution to the garden life that we *can* see and enjoy.

Know your soil

Understanding your soil's composition will encourage you to embrace aeration as a central part of your lawn care programme.

- Soil is made up of solids, liquids and gases.

A health soil comprises 50% solids (including approximately 5% organic matter), 25% water and 25% air.

- If your soil is compacted, it can be as much as 90% solid with only 5% each of water and air – not conducive to plant growth!

- The soil beneath your grass has three layers: 1) topsoil - where most of the organic matter, nutrients and organisms can be found, 2) subsoil - where most of the water is stored, and 3) parent material – the underlying geological bedrock or drift deposit which gives the soil many of its mineral and structural characteristics.

And here are some more facts to inspire even more respect for the soil:

grass

topsoil

subsoil

- Nature's own strategy to prevent compaction is to grow plants! Healthy roots loosen the soil as they grow, allowing water and oxygen to penetrate. This in turn benefits both the plants themselves and the soil organisms.

- Maintaining a healthy environment for micro-organisms is important; it is the bacteria in the soil which can help convert nutrients into usable plant food for the grass.

- Soil is said to store approximately 0.01% of the Earth's water within its pores and cracks.

Looking after your soil

You can see I am a fan of soil - and I hope you can now appreciate how vital soil is to good lawn care. However, making *big* changes to your soil is extremely difficult - whatever we have in our garden is pretty much what we have to work with. Keeping soil healthy is more an exercise in mindful maintenance, and the two issues which occupy gardeners the most are soil pH and soil structure.

1. The pH factor

Many of us will remember 'pH' from our school days, but we may have forgotten what it means! Quite simply, pH is a measurement of acidity/alkalinity. A pH of 7 is described as neutral, neither acidic nor alkaline (for example, pure water); a pH reading above 7 is said to be alkaline, and one below 7 is said to be acidic. With soil, the pH can theoretically be anything from 1 to 14.

The pH of your soil will affect its biological, chemical and physical properties which, in turn, affect the plants growing in it. However, adjusting your soil's pH is very difficult and it's better to think in terms of *compensating* for any problems relating to your soil's pH. If you are determined to change the pH, be warned that it is often very hard work and gives only a small and often temporary change.

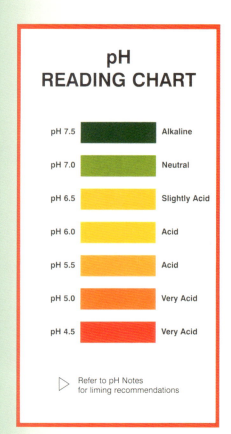

pH
READING CHART

pH 7.5	Alkaline
pH 7.0	Neutral
pH 6.5	Slightly Acid
pH 6.0	Acid
pH 5.5	Acid
pH 5.0	Very Acid
pH 4.5	Very Acid

▷ Refer to pH Notes
for liming recommendations

Testing your pH

This is the easy part. You can buy pH meters in any garden centre and, whilst not as accurate as laboratory equipment, they're good enough for our purposes. Whether your lawn is acid or alkaline, a very high or low reading will indicate one possible problem - the grass may not be accessing sufficient nutrients as they may be locked in by the soil. There can also be other problems associated with the two sides of the pH coin.

Acid soil (below pH7)

Sometimes referred to as 'sour soil', acid soil can be a tough environment for some plants. However, its effect in lawns is more apparent on the thatch (see p40). The acidity can slow down microbial activity leading to slower breakdown of the thatch.

Raising the pH requires an application of lime. In the past this powdered dressing was almost impossible to use for domestic purposes, but is now available as a granular fertiliser.

Alkaline soil (above pH7)

An alkaline soil will often suffer from excessive weed growth along with thriving coarser grasses within the mix. In this environment, the main grass types can struggle to compete for space and nutrients.

You can reduce the alkalinity a little by applying ferrous sulphate (moss killer) or sulphur-based products, but this only helps in the short term and should not be considered a long-term solution. However, fertilisers often contain sulphur, thereby feeding the lawn and slightly reducing the alkalinity at the same time.

2. Soil structure

The structure of each of the three layers of your lawn is continually changing. Within the soil this change is in the proportions of solids, water and air and can impact seriously on the grass above. However, we can monitor these changes and, to some extent, address any imbalance when necessary. We just need to appreciate that there is a cyclical relationship between what we can see on the surface and what is going on out of sight down below. This means that interventions we use to improve the grass will inevitably have some knock-on effect on the soil. Get the interventions right and you can simultaneously look after the entire triple-layer structure, above and below ground.

For example, *everyday traffic* across the lawn will compress the soil below, squeezing out vital air and making life much harder for the delicate roots within the soil. Now, we may not be able to control or change the traffic, but we can understand just how important aeration (p64) is in mitigating this and restoring air pockets within the soil structure.

The *weather* is another thing we can't control but we *can* understand what it does and respond accordingly. Heavy rain combined with compaction will squeeze out much of the essential air, so remedial action may have to be increased to compensate. And of course, in prolonged dry periods, the soil will shrink, leaving the roots exposed and slowly dying for want of water and nutrients. Good thatch control (see Scarification p98) will help to give the soil a protective and nurturing layer, better able to withstand the extremes of our changing climate.

So, while it may hide away out of sight, the soil plays a vital part in the health of our lawns; and while it may not be exposed like the surface grass it is just as vulnerable to the same challenges of climate and wear and tear. And most importantly, if things go wrong down below, it's not long before we see the effects of this on the surface. However, get your routine lawn care programme right and you will be doing much of what is needed to maintain a healthy soil.

discussion

Q: Why is it so important to aerate the soil?

A stale soil, starved of oxygen, will grow a stale lawn. Soils are there to work for us but we need to help them along. Aeration is the best way to do this. Remember a famous political leader's answer to the question "What are your three top policies?" My answer (and that of every turf manager in the world) would be "aeration, aeration and aeration".

Hollow-tine aerating maintains healthy soil

Q: Are there spin-off benefits to working my soil?

Yes, of course! Improving your soil (principally by aerating) will automatically get your soil more active by encouraging all your soil bacteria and organisms. This in turn helps break down thatch more quickly and aids root strength, making your grass look healthier.

Q: I have poor clay soil; what can I do?

It very much depends on just how 'poor'. Ask yourself, does the grass grow reasonably well? And are you doing enough to keep it healthy? If so, then I shouldn't worry. Some people are tempted to add complex drainage systems, or even replace the soil entirely. Don't even think about that until you are sure you really have put in place a good routine lawn care programme - it is perfectly possible to maintain a decent domestic lawn on relatively inadequate soil.

Q: Should I add sand to my heavy soil?

Using sand is a tricky intervention. You can't just use any old sand (see my discussion about sand in Aeration, p64) and if you use too much, the soil will dry out too quickly and you'll have to resort to an expensive irrigation system. Choosing the correct sand is imperative, so it's best to contact a soil/top dressing specialist for help assessing the problem.

Q: My soil is very sandy and free draining. What can I do to help it retain moisture?

This is the opposite problem to a clay soil! Sand has difficulty in retaining moisture and nutrients. I suggest you continue with essential scarification and aeration to maintain plant health. Slow-release organic feeds can aid microbial activity in sandy soils, which in turn will improve moisture and feed retention.

main
techniques

Contents:

Aeration | Mowing | Nutrition | Scarification | Watering

plus ADDITIONAL Techniques –

Laying new turf | Top dressing | Overseeding

aeration

"Look at that amazing grass; they must spend a fortune on fertiliser!" Many gardeners think this when observing well-kept sports venues or formal lawns. But they're wrong. The single most important contributor to this fabulous grass they're admiring is aeration.

On the domestic front, however, aeration is the most underrated part of the annual care programme. Admittedly, the professional lawn might typically be aerated more than twenty times a year - nearly twice a month - and I'm not suggesting you commit to that regime! But understanding why these experts do this, and the difference it makes, especially in today's climate, will encourage you to devote just a little time not just to aeration - but to the correct method of aeration, doing it for the right reason and valuing the tremendous difference it makes to the health of your lawn.

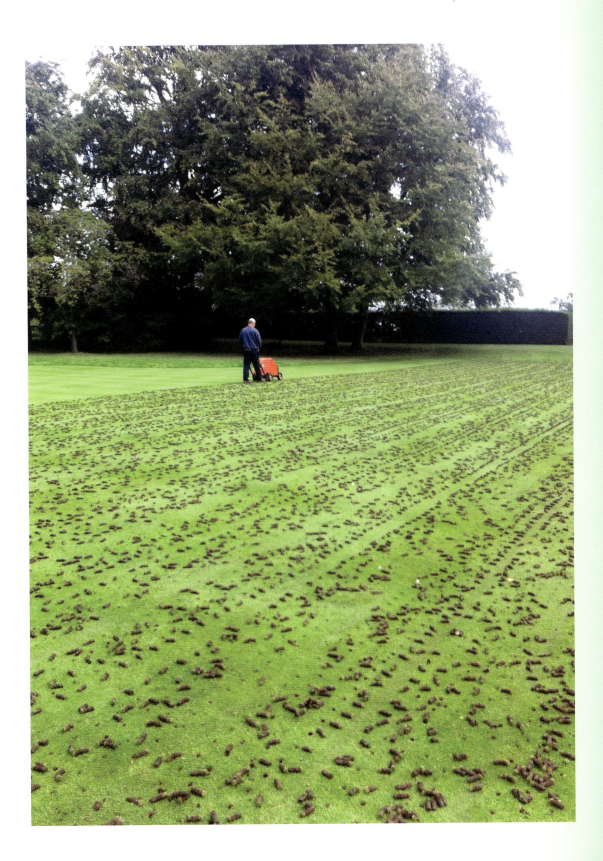

What IS aeration?

A healthy soil should be approximately 50% solids, 25% water and 25% air, but over time the air is slowly squeezed out. Aeration is the process of creating tiny channels from the surface down into the soil in order to let more air back into the root zone, restoring this balance and maintaining a healthy eco-system.

Why do we need to aerate?

Lawn grasses are delicate plants, easily stressed by compacted dry soils, waterlogged earth and the heat of the sun. Their roots need the optimum balance of solids, water and air in order to thrive. Microbial activity, essential to the prevention of excess thatch, also depends on a good supply of air. However, thanks to nature the soil's profile, structure and composition changes every single day; to maintain a healthy lawn, we have to try and keep up with this, and one the most important tasks is aeration.

Like most gardening techniques, aeration is not a precise science. The benefits of aeration are sometimes slow to take effect - you may not see the obvious improvements for a few months - but it is still a valuable way for everyone from turf professionals to domestic gardeners to help maintain a healthy lawn system.

Poor aeration is the principle reason for unhealthy lawns

Immediately after aerating (and scarifying)   *A few weeks later*

What to expect after aerating

You are unlikely to see immediate benefits from your aerating, but good things *will* be happening. Cracks will have been created to allow more air entry and circulation; bacteria will be increasing; and most important of all, the grass plants will be growing more strongly with a healthy root system.

Patience and faith are essential! Unlike some lawn care tasks, aerating simply seems to create a mess of small soil clumps and holes strewn all over the grass. This may be one of the reasons why it is so neglected, but it is essential work. And an average lawn (250m2) can take less than an hour both to aerate and then to clear the cores from the lawn. Compare this to the time we spend mowing!

Eventually, however, you *will* see the results, not as a sudden revelation but as the joint outcome of your combined lawn care programme. Why not take 'before' and 'after' photos six months or even a year apart? Regardless of the rainfall and the impact of your feeding and scarifying programmes, if you aerate you will know that it has contributed significantly to the healthy green sward you will be admiring.

Keep in mind why you're doing it!

How to aerate your lawn

First, the bad news. Simply copying professional lawn care practice is not the ideal solution for domestic lawn care. The professionals typically use multiple aeration techniques AND do it far more often than we can reasonably manage.

Now, the good news. Until quite recently, many of us have relied on hard manual labour using ordinary or specialised forks to 'stick some holes in the ground'. But nowadays, with the availability of well-designed machines, why continue to use this back-breaking method? Garden centres and hire shops can provide the solution, and to minimise the cost, many people are beginning to share purchase or hire with their friends and neighbours. And, for those who really don't have the time, why not simply hire a local lawn care firm to do it for you?

Below I briefly describe the five main methods to choose from when aerating a domestic lawn (bearing in mind that you will not have the time that professionals can give to their lawns).

AERATION METHODS

Garden fork

Expert rating ✓

Using a garden fork adds air to the soil profile but is *incredibly hard work* and can damage the root systems if done incorrectly.

What it does: forking with a regular garden fork simply forces prong-shaped channels through the thatch and into the soil. This lets in air but also compacts the surrounding soil.

How: Reverse the fork and insert it without wiggling. Work in rows 2-4 inches apart.

TIP: Work in small, manageable areas – a little at a time. It is very hard work!

WARNING:
Do not wiggle the fork around once inserted (especially in frost) as this can cause significant root damage.

Hollow-tine fork

Expert rating ✓ ✓ ✓ ✓

Hollow-tine aeration is arguably the best method of all, and certainly best suited to the domestic lawn. Using a specially designed fork with hollow prongs, the manual method described here is a little easier than using a regular fork.

What it does: instead of forcing gaps into the soil which can compact the surrounding earth, hollow-tining actually removes part of the soil. The broader soil structure remains the same but now it has space for improved air and water movement as well as better root development.

How: Insert the fork into the ground in rows 2-4 inches apart, allowing the plugs of extracted soil to pop out at the top.

TIP: Use more closely in areas of greater compaction and wear (perimeters, walkways, etc).

courtesy of Bosmere Products

Hollow-tine machine

Expert rating ✓ ✓ ✓ ✓ ✓

Mechanical hollow-tining is by far the easiest and most effective aeration method. There are many types of machine but they all work, are simple to use and achieve all the benefits of manual hollow-tining without the hard labour!

What it does: as with the hollow-tine fork, the machines drive hollow prongs into the earth which force plugs of soil up, leaving behind channels but without compacting the surrounding soil. The results include excellent water percolation and drainage, strong root development and good fertiliser absorption.

How: Most machines are well designed with set speeds, set spacing and as few levers as possible. As the tines project into the ground, the machine automatically moves forward so you don't have to calculate or monitor distances.

TIP: Share the cost of machine purchase or hire with a neighbour – or even use a local lawn company. The results are worth it.

WARNING:
Try to follow straight lines when possible; machines which are designed to penetrate the ground don't like corners!

Slitting

Expert rating ✓ ✓ ✓

Slitting is an effective method for cutting through shoots and stolons which helps to thicken up some grass species, but it is not as effective for reducing compaction.

What it does: the mechanism creates tiny slits in the earth. These remain open, allowing air to enter and creating small crevices for roots and water to penetrate.

How: Machines differ (for example, some have weights to drive the tines deeper into the sward) so always follow the directions supplied. After slitting, the shoots and stolons will adjust their angle of growth so it is a good idea to vary the angle of attack each time you aerate.

TIP: Best used in conjunction with other aeration methods.

WARNING:
Be careful when turning to avoid damage to both the lawn and the machine.

Solid-tine

Expert rating ✓ ✓ ✓

Solid-tining is essentially a mechanical version of the good old garden fork. Its chief benefit is ease of use and good performance in the right soil conditions. However, solid-tining does not remove any soil or reduce compaction and while it certainly aerates the soil, it is not well suited to the domestic lawn.

What it does: the machine drives solid tines into the ground, allowing the air to penetrate. Providing the soil condition is good, this also encourages root development.

How: As with hollow-tine machines, these are well designed and easy to use. As always, follow the instructions that are supplied by the manufacturer.

TIP: Despite its limitations, solid-tine aeration is still thought of as a labour-saving option which may be the main priority for some gardeners.

WARNING: Simply driving a solid-tine into a lawn with serious compaction problems will not lead to a healthier sward. Either change your aeration method or consider additional measures to reduce the compaction.

When (and how often) to aerate

Aeration dries out the top surface, so in dry seasons there is a risk of drying out the soil as well. To avoid this, aerate only when the soil is moist, typically from September to April (slowing down from March onwards). Beware of an unusually dry spring, and avoid aerating during frost as this can cause root and tip damage.

In theory you can aerate as often as you like, but be guided by the chief aim - to reduce compaction in the soil without letting it dry out. And if bad weather knocks your schedule out of kilter, make adjustments rather than neglecting it.

When: The table below indicates the good months for each technique. For an indication of the frequency, refer to the notes that follow. If you have an irrigation system, you can prick and solid-tine beyond these dates to keep the water irrigation working.

	How often	J	F	M	A	M	J	J	A	S	O	N	D
Hollow-tining	1-3/year	√	√	√	√	×	×	×	×	√	√	√	√
Slitting	1-2/month	√	√	√	×	×	×	×	×	√	√	√	√
Solid-tining	1-2/month	√	√	√	√*	√*	√*	√*	√*	√	√	√	√
Pricking**		√	√	√	√	√	√	√	√	√	√	√	√

With solid-tining and slitting, use only as a secondary form of aeration in addition to hollow-tining. If your lawn is unhealthy you can increase frequency up to 3-4 times per month during appropriate times of year.

*From April to the end of August, shallow solid-tining can be done to help water penetration if you are irrigating.

***Pricking, which makes large numbers of holes in just the top surface, is much underrated and has two benefits:*

1) Helping create a seedbed for small repairs, and

2) Aiding penetration of water into the soil profile, either directly before watering or by allowing rain water to percolate through.

Pricking can be done with a garden fork (for small areas) or with a selection of pedestrian and towable tools.

Which method(s) should I use?

This depends on the quality of lawn you want to achieve. Below are three different aeration programmes ranging from the bare minimum to a complex intervention.

1)   (for a basic utility lawn) hollow-tine once a year, between September and March

2)   (for a quality lawn) hollow-tine once a year, and slit or solid-tine up to once a month from September to March

3)   (for a luxury lawn) hollow-tine 1-2 times a year, and alternate slitting and solid-tining up to once a month from September to March (and pricking as required)

NB: Although hollow-tining is generally done once or twice a year, some people like to do it more frequently, up to once a month. If you do this, use a pencil-tine (smaller diameter) to cause less surface disruption. It is also a good idea to apply a top dressing if you hollow-tine monthly.

discussion.

Q: "I've never aerated before; what are the most important things to consider?

Simple - it all comes down to good planning, timing and monitoring:

Plan! Thinking well ahead about when and how you plan to aerate will save you time by dovetailing around other garden work; it can also save you money if you plan to share equipment hire with a neighbour.

Timing Avoid aerating in mid-summer (May to August). Slitting late into May, for example, will create slits that remain open and bake hard in the summer sun, leading to moisture loss and the surface drying out.

Equally, avoid aerating when the ground is frozen or you will damage the root systems. If you just have a surface frost, wait until the white frost has thawed before aerating.

Monitor! Keep records of what you do, and when, and then note the outcomes later in the year. You don't want to waste effort just punching holes in the ground at random, hoping it is doing some good. By monitoring, you can discover what works best for your lawn, and feed this into your future planning.

Q: "Should I fill up the holes with sand?"

The simple answer is no, not as part of your aeration routine (unless you are producing a fine quality lawn, cut with a cylinder mower). Applying sharp sand is actually part of what we call a soil exchange process (see below) and is rarely needed for domestic lawns. Instead, sand should really only be used as part of a good quality soil/sand dressing mix (see Top Dressing 129).

Q: "Should I remove the cores from the surface?"

There are two ways to look at this. On one hand, leaving them there can create a mess in wet weather, putting the lawn out of bounds, and they can encourage disease. On the other hand, the cores are full of 'good' bacteria. It has taken time to build these up in the soil, so why take them away? The simple fact is that leaving them on the surface to break down naturally (or lending a hand if the weather isn't helping - for example with a scarifier set to work at ground level) will give the goodness back to the soil as a free, beneficial top dressing!

However, if you are planning a special top dressing (or you really do not like seeing your lawn covered with little plugs of soil, as in the picture) then by all means clear them up. Just bear in mind that if the weather is very wet, you might create an even bigger mess by trying to remove them.

The Great Sand Debate

The practice of adding sharp sand originates from the golf course environment where they use a process called 'soil exchange'. This process was developed for the old soil push-up green*, and was gradually replaced over many years to create more modern greens with finer grasses.

In domestic lawn care, we're always looking for ways to improve care whilst reducing labour and costs. As a result there is much debate about using sharp sand in dressings. Personally I don't favour it (except perhaps for very heavy soils) for a number of reasons.

Unless it has been tested for granule size and shape, pH, etc, we never know the exact quality of the sharp sand (builder's sharp sand is meant for building, not for lawns), and...

... the wrong type of grain size, shape etc can shear the roots, impede drainage (even making it wetter at times) alter the pH balance and even dry out the surface too much.

Why take away a bacterial-filled core (aerating) and replace it entirely with an inert material? Adding a 60:40 or 70:30 type blend of soil and sand will improve drainage as well as keeping up bacteria levels.

A 'soil push-up' type of green was an old form of golf course design whereby there was little or no drainage system. This meant that percolation through the soil profile was paramount. To encourage this percolation, golf greens had hollow tine plugs removed and the holes filled with shard sand. To this day, it is still done to maintain older greens.

mowing

INCLUDES: Mowing heights; mowing frequency; mowing technique; edging and clipping

(See also All About Mowers, p228)

Mowing is the one thing you will do most frequently and it's the one thing you can't neglect without the evidence being clearly visible to all! However, mowing is less to do with neat parallel stripes and more to do with sustaining good lawn health. Fortunately a few guiding principles, some time commitment and a well-maintained mower are all that you need for an effective and manageable mowing regime.

How short should I cut? And how often?

These are the two most commonly-asked questions about mowing. For many gardeners the answer to the second will be to mow more often than you might think. And it is the answer to the *first* which dictates just how often. For cutting grass, there is actually a very simple rule of thumb - never cut more than one third of the current length; if you do, you risk harming the plant's natural ability to store food and water. But of course to make sense of this rule we need to know what our *target* length should be - and this depends on the type of grass, the grade of lawn and the time of year, as explained below.

Mowing heights
- what is the ideal height?

The ideal height of your newly-cut grass can depend on the mix of species in your lawn. Grass (p24) explains how to identify these, and although the ratio of constituent plants will be constantly changing, knowing the most prevalent species can help you select the best cutting height.

Most lawns are either blends of bents and fescues or principally dwarf ryegrass with some bents and fescues mixed in. For the best results, these two types need different cutting heights, reflecting their different growing habits.

NB: In the **table opposite** I have created *three* categories of lawn by dividing the Utility Lawn into two categories - Low Quality (a basic, healthy everyday lawn) and Medium Quality (with the robustness of a utility lawn but a better finish).

Bents and fescues lawn

This, the traditional British lawn, is more labour-intensive than the newer dwarf ryegrass lawns. Used on golf courses, these native grasses can withstand very close cutting, necessary for a perfect ball-roll. However, on the domestic lawn, cutting too short will add to your overall lawn maintenance by creating more dead material which increases the thatch levels. On the other hand, if left uncut for too long, these grasses naturally develop more shoots and leaves as they grow, which in turn will also add to the thatch layer.

So, choose your height plan and try to stick to it! And remember, one of the benefits of bents and fescues is their natural dense growing habit. Regular mowing will encourage this behaviour, helping to maintain a full and even covering.

Suggested heights

High quality lawn (typically cylinder mown)

Spring	15mm
Summer	10mm
Autumn	15mm
Winter	20mm

Medium quality lawn (rotary)

Spring	20mm
Summer	20mm
Autumn	20mm
Winter	20mm

Low quality lawn (rotary)

Spring	30mm
Summer	30mm
Autumn	30mm
Winter	30mm

Majority dwarf ryegrass lawn

Dwarf ryegrass is a species bred deliberately for the domestic lawn - but this does not mean it is easier to maintain, just different. The main points to bear in mind are:

- The characteristic deep green colour is in the leaf blade, so removing too much can weaken the appearance
- Keeping a slightly longer grass length will maintain the lush thickness of ryegrass, ideal for a hard-wearing lawn
- The grass is more abrasive so you will need to sharpen the mower blades more often.

Apart from these, the mowing demands are slightly more than those of a bent and fescue lawn. If you look carefully you will see some difference in ideal seasonal heights.

Suggested heights

High quality lawn (possibly cylinder mown)

Spring	20mm
Summer	15mm
Autumn	20mm
Winter	25mm

Medium quality lawn (rotary)

Spring	20mm
Summer	20mm
Autumn	25mm
Winter	30mm

Low quality lawn (rotary)

Spring	35mm
Summer	35mm
Autumn	35mm
Winter	35mm

Mowing frequency
- how often should I mow?

Your own lawn is unique in its grass blend, micro-climate, location, soil, thatch etc – and so you really need to establish a regime that works best for you; and that means keeping notes of what you do and of how it all turns out (see tips in 12-Month Programme, p224)!

Start by using the target lengths above as an indication of when you need to mow; keep a record and also note unusual weather, feeds and other treatments and any problems arising directly from the mowing (thinning grass, moss, dry patches etc). Mid-winter, when garden activity is at its quietest, is a good time to review and revise your programme for the year ahead.

Below is a guide to the *frequency* of mowing you should anticipate:

January	1-2 cuts per month
February	1-2 cuts per month
March	2-4 cuts per month
April	2-4 cuts per month
May	4-8 cuts per month
June	4-8 cuts per month
July	4-8 cuts per month
August	4-8 cuts per month
September	2-6 cuts per month
October	2-4 cuts per month
November	1-4 cuts per month
December	1-2 cuts per month

Mowing technique
- establishing a consistent method

Before you mow, there are two important checks to be done.

Firstly, check the mower. Make sure it has the correct lubricants and that the blade is sharp - and of course check the height of the blade to ensure you don't cut more than one-third of the leaf-blade. You can find useful information about your mower in the Appendix (p228).

Secondly, check the lawn itself. Once you begin mowing you will be using your distant vision to keep you straight and will not be able to examine the ground right in front of you. So before you start to mow, check the ground for debris, twigs, stones, toys etc and make a note of any problems which will soon need attention.

Before you start mowing, it is a good idea to do your edging. The mower can then collect up some of the edging clippings as you do your perimeter cut (see below).

Now you're ready to start mowing. This is the routine I use once I've completed my two preliminary checks and my edging:

1. Cut the perimeter two or three strips deep so that you give yourself more turning space at each end of the lawn.

2. Choose the direction in which you want to mow (and if you are striping your lawn, move the mower to the centre before you begin the main cut).

3. Pick a fixed point in the distance and walk towards it as you mow, but do not take your eyes from it until you reach the end.

4. After turning at the other end of this pass, align the mower to slightly overlap the last pass.

5. Walk back down the lawn on your next pass, but stand to the side of the machine that you made your last pass on. This way you will find it easier to keep that straight line.

6. Continue to do this until you have finished one side of the lawn.

7. Complete the rest of the lawn, in the same manner.

8. When completed, do another tidy up pass on the perimeter cuts.

9. Each mowing day, try to alternate the direction of each straight line; this will prevent 'graining' where the grass grows in one specific direction.

10. Now, before you sit down to admire your newly-cut lawn, go and wash down that mower (and maybe collect up any clippings left behind by your mower).

Edging and Clipping

A neatly-clipped edge provides the perfect crisp finish to a newly-cut lawn. I actually find it easier to do this before I mow; this way some of the cuttings can be collected by the mower. Some people, however, prefer to leave it to the end, enjoying it as the final, rewarding step in the mowing process. Fortunately, whether edging routinely after mowing or to creating a new outline to the lawn, there's no great secret or skill.

Routine maintenance edging
You should be doing this on a weekly basis - but don't worry, there are good tools to make it easy! Whichever you choose, the process is the same, working your way around the edge of the lawn. Just remember, all cutting tools need to be kept sharp!

Clippers
This is the standard manual tool. With good sharp blades it is very effective and easy to use. Some people find it almost therapeutic with its gentle but precise action and peaceful snipping sound.

Reciprocator
The reciprocator is our solution for mechanising the manual clippers. It is ideal for the slightly larger area. Strapped to your shoulder, its blade does all the hard work for you and, being adjustable, it should need sharpening less frequently too. As with the clippers, the cutting action comes from two blades passing against each other, so the finish is very sharp.

Strimmer
The versatile strimmer is so adaptable! By pivoting the head on its swivel axis, it is instantly converted into an easy-to-use edging tool. Be aware though that because it relies on the plastic cord, the finish will not be quite as good as using twin blades.

Reshaping the lawn edge

Technically still an edging task, creating or tidying up an edge is somewhat harder than routine edging. And again, it relies on having the right tools.

Manual Edging Iron

This is the familiar half-moon implement with a sharp edge to cut through the thatch and soil and create clean edging lines. Easy to use, it's best for smaller areas and more intricate shapes.

Pedestrian Edger

These machines are designed to help you create a clean edge over a much longer distance. They also remove a larger piece of turf than the manual tool.

If using an old hosepipe, peg it down to prevent it from moving out of place

Both tools will do the same basic job and are easy to use. Less easy can be the process of marking out the new edge before you begin - which is crucial to getting a good clean result! The simplest ways to do this is by using:

- a hosepipe or a piece of string (for manual edging iron only)

- flour or sand to mark out your line

- turf paint to mark out your line.

Warning! When creating your new shape, remember to consider the mower and any other machine you plan to use on the lawn. You may have to compromise your design to accommodate a realistic turning circle.

discussion.

Q: If the grass is growing quickly, how often should I cut?

Once a week is usually fine but in the heaviest periods of grass growth (e.g. March and September) you may want to cut twice a week. And I would suggest a routine such as mowing, say, on a Tuesday with the box *off* and Friday with the box *on*.

Q: How do I set the right mower height?

Essentially there are two ways - follow the instructions in the user manual, and use your own observations. Did the lawn look healthy after the last cut? Did it look scalped and too short? It's always better to start higher and reduce the height in small increments over several cuts. Also remember that your thatch layer may affect the actual cutting height if the mower sinks into it, bringing the blade closer to the grass.

Q: Which mower should I choose for my lawn?

Mowers are like cars - all very different but essentially doing the same thing. Some mowers have two wheels and a roller, some have four wheels and some have none and hover instead - but they all cut grass and they all have some kind of blade (not always sharp enough though). If you want stripes, you need a roller mower; if you want the most perfect, exquisite lawn you need a cylinder mower, but if you just want a healthy, usable lawn, choose a good 4-wheeled mower. You can find more information about mowers in the Appendix (p228).

Q: Are plastic blades suitable?

Whilst they will cut, it must be remembered that they will not cut as sharply or cleanly as well-maintained metal blades.

Q: How long should my blade last?

Even with regular sharpening, after a time, blades become unbalanced. A good blade-sharpening routine should see two blades last up to and sometimes more than 24 months. (For advice on sharpening, see the Appendix, p234)

Q: Should I mow when it's wet?

Mowing is best done when conditions are dry - you get a cleaner cut and don't create sticky mud. But rain shouldn't be an excuse not to mow at all, especially if you then end up with ankle-deep grass! And, if you have a compost bin and miss out on the mowing for weeks on end, you're losing all that wonderful energy from the grass cuttings.

Mowing wet grass is fine provided your blades are kept really sharp, otherwise you'll just tear the grass (it's just like wet shaving - efficient if the razor is sharp, but a nasty experience if not). And if you hit on a glorious sunny winter's day, go out mid-morning and remove the dew using a broom or a blower; then by mid-afternoon the lawn will be much drier, giving you ideal mowing conditions even in the middle of winter!

Above: Blunt Right: Sharp

NB: New blades don't come ready-sharpened - you will need to sharpen them before use

nutrition

INCLUDES: Why grass needs food; the basics of fertilisers; which fertiliser to choose; how to feed and how often.

Look at a professionally maintained lawn – green, lush and healthy throughout the year! One reason for this can be nutrition, a carefully-tailored 12-month feeding programme. After all, grass is a plant which keeps growing on and off throughout the year so it shouldn't be any surprise that it enjoys a good feed. However, most domestic gardeners feed their lawn once a year, maybe twice, and, if other key techniques are not routinely used, even this can be a wasted effort as the grass is unable to derive the full benefit. So, to get the best from a nutrition regime, we need to address the basic questions – why feed, what to feed and when to feed – and then incorporate this into our 12-month lawn programme.

Why grass needs food

Grass plants draw on dozens of different nutrients and elements in their environment to survive and thrive. However by far the most important of these are nitrogen (N), phosphorus (P) and potassium (K). These are used up quickly and need replenishing in the form of N-P-K fertilisers. Each component element helps the plant in a different way:

Nitrogen helps to promote sturdy plants, giving strong shoots and leaves and dense growth which helps reduce competition from weeds.

Phosphorus helps the grass to establish and grow strong root systems.

Potassium reduces the impact of stress on the plant by giving it resistance to disease, drought, wear and tear and cold weather.

Feeding the correct mixture of these three elements and at the right times of year will ensure the grass always has the optimum supply of each when it needs it most. This means devising a balanced programme which reflects the plants' needs rather than our own convenience, but it is much easier than you might think if you use the guidelines that follow.

The basics of fertilisers

The most important thing to understand about fertiliser is how the grass uses it - otherwise you can throw the stuff at your lawn with little positive impact. Here are some important basic facts:

When we mow we are removing parts of the plant which store the food - the leaves - hence the need to provide additional nutrition.

For the roots to absorb nutrients oxygen is needed in a usable form - hence the need for aeration to avoid compaction and maintain drainage.

All fertiliser mixes have a predefined effective life once applied - some last for six weeks, some for six months (you will find information about this on the packets). The shorter-lasting ones work more quickly on the grass but then run out. The longer-term ones will have some of the fast initial action but are mostly a slower-release food. This all needs to be considered when planning your programme and selecting your fertilisers.

The ratio of the three key elements (N, P & K) changes at different times of the year, reflecting the different needs of the plant. This is why you need to feed different mixes in different seasons. Manufacturers can also factor in different release speeds - for example, quick-release for cold weather when a faster action may be required.

Where fertilisers come from

The three elements appear in the fertilisers as compounds, most commonly urea and various nitrates for nitrogen, assorted phosphates for the phosphorus and potassium chloride for the potassium. The actual choice of compound varies around the world depending on local availability and the different ways that they behave in the soil as they are broken down and absorbed by the plants.

Which fertiliser to choose

This means you must try to select the right fertiliser accordingly, but as there is no rule of thumb I suggest starting with moderate quantities and monitoring the results. The product information will include the ratio of nitrogen to phosphorus to potassium (N-P-K) - usually as three numbers like these: 5-5-10, 4-0-10 (where '0' indicates nil phosphorus in the mix), etc. If this sounds complicated, don't worry! Just use the following as a guideline.

	fescue/bent lawn	ryegrass lawn
season	Which N-P-K ratio?	Which N-P-K ratio?
SPRING (eg March)	5-5-10 (25g/m^2)	5-5-10 (35g/m^2)
SUMMER (eg June)	10-5-5 (25g/m^2)	10-5-5 (30g/m^2)
AUTUMN (eg September)	16-5-10 (25g/m^2)	16-5-10 (30g/m^2)
WINTER (eg December)	4-0-10 + FE (25g/m^2)	4-0-10 + FE (25g/m^2)

Notice the addition of FE (iron) in the winter mix, and the different application. rates for a dwarf ryegrass lawn.

Pure fertilisers *vs* 'feed and weed' mixes

It is quite natural to be tempted by the combined fertiliser and weed killer mixes - they promise to do two jobs in one, after all! And they do work to an extent. However they are always a compromise compared to separate applications of each and, because of the risks of over-application, they are not as strong as their individual equivalents and so have less effect. You can read more about this topic in Weed Control, p144.

Some extra tips

Do NOT use slow-release fertilisers for an early spring start. The coatings are designed to take longer to wear away.

When using FE (iron), try to use it as a separate product (eg for moss control). If you buy a fertiliser specifically because it contains FE it will only be for a 'colour-up'.

Don't use products with FE during summer or hot, dry periods.

After seeding, apply high phosphate feeds (6-18-6 for example).

Towards autumn/winter use high potassium feeds.

Avoid late autumn feeds with too high a nitrogen content.

How to feed - and how often

Granular vs liquid

In professional lawn care, you might find a liquid feed being applied every 4-6 weeks, with the product and ratios being varied throughout the year. In the 'real world' this is an unrealistic gardening commitment, and accurate liquid application is difficult due to different sprayer calibrations and varying water pressure.

So I recommend 4-6 granular feeds a year using products that last for approximately 12 weeks (see 'Once or twice?' below). It is much easier to apply granules accurately and they will provide a steady feed of nutrients to the grass as they break down and are absorbed into the soil. You can turn to liquid feeds (which are absorbed much more quickly) as 'top-ups' if, for example, your granules have been washed away prematurely by heavy rain.

Once or twice per season?

Check the product for information on how long the fertiliser remains active. If it is a short-term one, you will need to repeat the feed during the season. However, with all products, try to overlap the applications to avoid dips in nutrient levels - for example, if your feed's instructions say it lasts for 12 weeks, reapply after nine or ten weeks.

Be careful not to over-feed, especially in wet months, as this will create too much top growth at the expense of strong root development.

Mechanical applicators

For accurate application you can use a machine. There are many to choose from but the drop spreaders are best used for combined 'feed and weed' products (especially when close to flower bed), while the spinning disc machines are ideal for fertilisers.

If you apply unevenly you will probably see streaks or scorching in the lawn. To avoid this, apply in two different directions, using half-strength quantities (as you are effectively going over the lawn twice). Remember, however, that moss killer and even weed killer, used incorrectly, can also scorch the grass.

Weather conditions

All fertilisers require washing in in order to activate. Those not containing a moss killer can be left to do this naturally when it next rains. However, those that do contain a moss killer often need water as soon as possible to prevent any scorching, so try to apply when you know that rain is imminent.

discussion

Q: Is it safe for children, pets and wildlife on the lawn after fertilising?

If you have used fertiliser on its own, then yes, you can walk on it immediately. However, if you have used anything containing weed killer or moss killer, you should play safe by keeping off the lawn until the rain has washed it in.

Q: Should I water straight after feeding?

This depends on what you have used. If you have used a straight fertiliser on its own, then you don't need to, although it can help to activate the feed. If you have used a feed and moss killer mix, then you must definitely water to prevent the moss killer from scorching the grass (unless you used a liquid application). If you have a feed and weed killer mix it is more complicated; watering can wash away any weed killer before it has chance to act, but some brands actually require water to release the feed granules from beneath the outer coating of weed killer. So, refer to the product instructions.

Q: What about mowing before and after fertilising?

When you use a fertiliser by itself you can mow a day before you apply and from a couple of day afterwards. When you mow afterwards, you want to avoid removing the fertiliser accidentally. Try leaving your box off and even raising the cutting height a little. It will only be a very light cut but keeps things under control until the fertiliser has been fully absorbed.

If you use a mix with weed killer, it is best not to mow for two to three days before and afterwards. You want the weeds to show plenty of leaf blade for the weed killer to attach itself to and, once applied, you need the leaves to remain intact while the killer takes effect.

Q: I've been recommended seaweed. Why?

Some liquid feeds contain seaweed and iron as colourants. They're great to use a week or so before a special event like a wedding as they can give the grass a wonderful rich green in a short space of time.

Q: What about organics?

Organics can be used - and can be excellent as they also work on the soil. They can sometimes be slightly odorous and can require slightly higher application rates. The only other downside can be an increase in worm casts due to the increase in soil microbes - but when that indicates good things going on in the soil, is it such a problem?

An organic fertiliser

scarification

INCLUDES: When to scarify; how to scarify; renovation scarification

Scarification *[n]: the removal of organic matter (dead matter and moss) from around the stem of the grass plant to maintain a healthy growing environment above and below the surface.*

Many gardeners only think about scarifying when they see the most visible sign of a problem - moss. By then, it becomes 'fire-fighting', an overdue response to a problem that has been allowed to reach unnecessary severity. The clever approach is to control the thatch in order to make it harder for the moss to take hold in the first place. As well as removing moss, scarifying also cleans out dead grass and weeds, and will actually help your lawn to thicken up, reviving the shoots and stolons. We just need to know when to do it and how to do it and then add it to our 12-month programme.

The good news is that thanks to modern tools, scarifying is not a horrendous task and, as this chapter explains, you can even get away with doing it as little as once a year!

When to scarify

Think of scarifying as a 'spring clean', (although you can also do it in the autumn) encouraging regrowth and renewed thickening during the warmer weather. Spring is generally the best time for a heavy scarification to remove a lot of material as scarifying heavily too late in the autumn (beyond September) can leave you with an open and muddy sward for many months. A light autumnal scarification, however, can be pushed as late as October. This rejuvenates British grasses by helping them to thicken back up again.

Which months are best? As with other interventions which disrupt the integrity of the lawn structure, we need to factor in recovery time. Without this, you may not see the wonderful benefit of thicker, lusher grass.

March/April or September are the best months for routine maintenance scarification - especially if the grass is thin, in poor condition or having a tough time with moss. If summer is going to be late or unusually wet, you can sometimes push into May. Similarly, an Indian summer and long autumn can open up October, but beware incoming cold and frosts.

How regularly? Some people scarify every two or three years, but you should aim to do it every year. As with all things in lawn care, little and often works best! I guarantee that the benefits will more than justify the effort. Instead of having to go in hard and remove a lot of material (which may then necessitate seeding and top dressing), you will be in much better control of the thatch and moss and enjoy a faster recovery time too. Your lawn will look great in just a few weeks.

TOP TIP: When scarifying, try to make two passes across the lawn for a better result.

A regularly scarified lawn will discourage problems like moss (compare with photo on p103)

How to scarify

The objective of scarification is not to remove *all* the thatch as this would eventually leave you with no grass either. So, if you have any lingering moss after scarifying, you will need to use moss killer.

The basic choice is between a manual hand-tool (a rake) and a pedestrian (non-self-propelling) machine.

Hand raking

'More effort for less benefit' sums up this option, although for very small areas it may be the only option. The rule is to go gently! Raking isn't just hard work; it also tugs away at good, healthy grass and even at the shallow roots. If you have to rake, you might want to consider a mechanised wire rake (see below) although these also risk removing too much healthy grass. Blades, by comparison, cut through the grass rather than pulling.

Pedestrian machines

There are lots of scarifying machines to choose from and they make the work much easier by using blades to slice through the thatch and moss. However there are different types of blade too and while some machines can have interchangeable blades, others (such as those for hiring) don't always give you an option. Therefore you need to know how each type's blade works.

Flail blade

This is the heaviest type of blade suitable for domestic use and it takes few prisoners! Great for scarifying really heavy thatch and dense moss, the blade also softens the turf, making it easier to comb out the debris using a more delicate machine or blade.

Fixed blade

A little thinner and less heavy than the flail, the fixed blade is ideal for maintaining good thatch levels and for simply combing out light moss.

Free-swinging blade

As with its fixed cousin, the free-swinging blade is good for general thatch maintenance and light combing, although it won't remove quite as much material (unless you do several passes).

Wire blade

This is basically a mechanised version of the wire rake and is useful for removing very light material but nothing more.

Flail blade

Fixed blade

Above: Free-swinging blade

Below: Mechanised wire blade

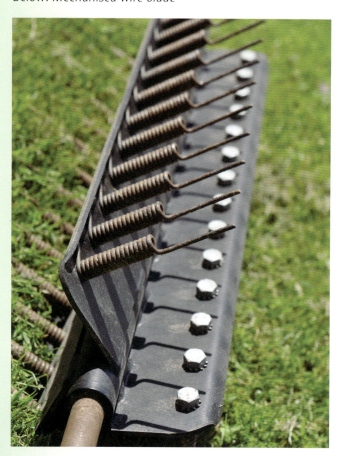

Which blade should I choose? My advice is always to start with a gentler blade. Monitor the results and only choose a tougher machine if you have to. Scarification is actually quite a brutal process so it's best to set the machine just off the ground and go over each area several times, gently combing out the material. It is more efficient than it sounds - with each pass you will be softening the thatch which lets the scarifier sit fractionally lower on the next pass and remove a little more material (so you won't necessarily have to lower the blades).

With a lot of moss you may need to go in harder, but remember that a lawn which has not been scarified for a long time will need a few seasons before you are completely in control of your thatch and moss. Nevertheless, you *will* still see improvements along the way!

Buy or hire? Both options are cheaper if you share the cost with a neighbour. If you are new to scarification, or need to do a severe renovation scarification to kick-start your annual programme, I recommend you find a good hire shop. As you become more confident, you can consider buying your own machine.

If it's really bad…

If your lawn is in very poor condition you may find the majority components are thatch and moss, with a good proportion of weeds too. If so, you need 'renovation scarification'! It is the most severe scarifying intervention and, not surprisingly, requires the longest recovery period. Some people imagine the massacre that is about to take place on their lawn and just decide not to do it, but this is a huge mistake. It *will* look dramatic and it *will* take longer for the lawn to recover, but the results will eventually pay off.

Technique

Every lawn is different - so the first task is to examine your thatch layer and assess the moss or thatch problem (see 'Thatch' p40 and 'Moss' p153). But if, say, your lawn has not been scarified for at least three years, my advice would be to start with a flail blade to loosen up the turf. Then either continue with the flail but more gently, or (if you can get away with it) use a lighter, free-swinging blade, a fixed or even a wire blade. Aim to leave as much grass behind as you can - it will then fill back more quickly.

discussion

Q: Should I cut the grass before scarifying?

Yes! In fact, this is the only time that I would recommend cutting the grass shorter than usual - this will remove more of the leaf blade, making it easier for the scarifier to remove the thatch and moss.

Q: Do I scarify in the same direction that I mow?

A good question, and generally I advise against this if you usually follow the same mowing pattern. Try to scarify by crossing the mowing line diagonally, even at two different angles. This gives you a better slicing action on the shoots and stolons which may be growing in the same direction as your mowing line.

Q: Should I feed the lawn afterwards?

Definitely! The aim of removing all that dead thatch and moss is to get all those wonderful grasses thickening back up before the moss and weeds can get back in. So, giving the grass a helping hand to revitalise makes good sense. Use your 12-month planner to synchronise this with your spring or autumn feed.

Q: Should I top dress the lawn after scarifying?

Top dressing (see p128) is not always required for a lawn of average quality (it's more important for luxury lawns). However, if you need to remove a lot of material (or do so accidentally), you *can* apply a seed and a top quality turf dressing to help it recover more quickly. This is also useful if you are trying to introduce new grass species into the lawn.

If you don't want to apply a top dressing, then try to remove less material this time round in your spring scarification, let it recover sooner by itself (with a feed - see above) and then scarify again later in the year.

Q: Should I use a box on the scarifier?

No, not usually. If you are using a domestic scarifer and taking out the correct amount of material, you'll just find it fills up far too quickly, doubling the time and effort you'll have to put in. They can also overbalance, and the weight of the contents can interfere with the scarifying action. Just leave the material to fall behind the machine as you move forwards.

Q: What's the best way to collect the debris when I've finished?

You don't want to disturb the surface any more than you have already, so just use a blower, a gentle rake or a besom.

Q: What can I do with the debris I've collected?

If you have a very mossy lawn, most of the debris will be moss. This doesn't break down easily in compost but you can add it little by little. Alternatively, moss makes very good hanging basket material - or even bedding for small domestic pets.

watering your lawn

INCLUDES: The impact of rain and drought; getting the most out of rainfall; when and how to water; watering newly seeded or turfed lawns

Approximately 20% of the Earth is covered with grass - and there's a good reason for this. Grass plants are brilliant survivors in all kinds of climates and weather patterns. However, our domestic lawns need some additional help to stop them from reverting to grass plains and wild meadows - and with our changing weather patterns, the big question is whether to water the lawn and, if so, how best to do this.

Green or keen?

Today's gardeners tend to fall into two camps - those who regard water as a valuable resource that requires preservation (the 'greens') and those who want their lawn to get the very best treatment possible (the 'keens'). If we didn't mind months of dry, scorched grass or boggy, waterlogged turf, we could just let nature take care of it. But some of us do mind; we want our lawn to remain as healthy as possible and to look good all year round. For *both* groups, the key is to understand the impact of rainfall and to optimise this before resorting to watering.

The impact of rain and drought

There is an amazing phenomenon which we all witness in our gardens most years - the gradual dying back and browning of the grass during the hot months followed by the miraculous return of lush, green grass! It has less to do with rainfall and more to do with the soil (see 'Soil' p52). A balanced soil has approximately 50% solids, 25% water and 25% air. Whilst this composition is constantly changing, it can do so drastically during both drought and excessive rain with a knock-on effect on the tiny root systems beneath the grass plants.

The cycle of nature

It's helpful to remember that grass is like any other living thing - eventually it dies! But a lawn is made up of thousands of individual plants, all at different stages in their lifecycle. Stress such as drought takes its toll on the older plants and on creeping grasses such as bents whose fragile roots don't penetrate deeper than the thatch. But there are always younger, fitter plants to take their place.

So, even in a really hot, dry period, the scorched lawn is not completely dead; it will recover. And the better you maintain the lawn environment using scarification and aeration, the stronger the recovery will be.

Do we get enough rain?

The 21st century is a period of huge climatic change and the instinct is to worry about *dryness* in the garden. But take a look at these figures from the Met Office concerning average annual rainfall between 1981 and 2010:

UK Area	Average number of days with rainfall exceeding 1mm	Average annual rainfall
Aberdeen (NE Scotland)	138.6	814.9mm
Glasgow (W Scotland)	170.3	1124.3mm
Southampton (S England)	114.7	779.4mm
Birmingham (Midlands/S England)	131.1	804.9mm
Manchester (N England)	151.7	867.1mm
Norwich (E England)	122.8	674.2mm
Belfast (N Ireland)	155.5	944.1mm
Cardiff (Wales)	148.6	1151.9mm

www.metoffice.gov.uk October 2013

While there is a big difference between Western Scotland and East Anglia, the country as a whole still enjoys plenty of wet days! The challenge is to make sure our lawns are in a condition best suited to benefit from this.

Getting the most out of rainfall

Helping your grass to get the most from rainfall is easy - it's just good lawn maintenance! Keeping your entire lawn structure as healthy as possible will ensure that neither drought nor deluge will do it any lasting damage.

Firstly, rain is of little use unless it penetrates where it is needed most. **Thatch control** will help maintain good water filtration through the sward and into the soil below (pricking may be useful to help the water to penetrate). Thatch control is also vital for reducing the drying and cracking in the hotter months, helping the soil to retain what little moisture it still has.

Secondly, grasses can't survive on water alone - so maintaining a healthy soil is important too. **Feeding** is important, as is routine **aeration** to help to maintain the oxygen, essential for the microbial activity which helps convert the food into nutrients for the grass.

When (and how) to water

Knowing when your lawn needs help

Wouldn't it be great if there was a simple test to indicate an equally simple remedy - watering? But it's not like that. It is far too easy either to overwater or to water inefficiently, so although brown and dry grass might look urgently in need of watering, unless you can guarantee it really needs it and that it will be effective, it is a waste of time and resources. So begin by checking the condition of the thatch; it may be that an otherwise adequate supply of rainfall is simply not getting through to the soil and roots below.

Another common mistake is to assume that, because you are already watering but seemingly without any great improvement, the grass must need *even more* watering. Note the temperature and wind conditions when you water - it may simply be that nature is intervening and absorbing it all back into the atmosphere (evapotranspiration).

Sometimes people use a pale colour in their lawn as an excuse to water it. It is more likely, however, that the weak colouring may indicate either excessive thatch or a nutrition deficiency (as in the picture below). Equally, raising the cutting height on the mower may be all that is needed to restore a healthy green colour!

If you do decide to water the lawn, take regular soil samples to monitor moisture levels in order to ensure that your work is effective. You may also need to keep notes of the time of day and weather conditions to determine which give you the best watering outcomes. And be sure you're ready for a sustained watering operation over the dry months - if you are inconsistent, then the results will be too.

Watering equipment

Lawn sprinkler: these come in many different forms but all work in essentially the same way. Great for covering large areas, you do however need to have good water pressure. It is difficult to use sprinklers with any accuracy, but they are good for watering newly laid turf (although they lack sufficient control for newly seeded areas).

Hand-held hose: for smaller lawns or to give some extra help to awkward areas and banks, this can be the most effective method and will ensure you don't waste any water. It is also ideal for newly-seeded areas (but remember to attach a fine rose first).

Technique

There are only three rules to observe when watering:

1) Avoid shallow or under-watering; this will simply cause shallow rooting and poor root development whilst possibly favouring the wrong species of grass. Make sure the water is penetrating well into the soil.

2) Don't water in the middle of the day. As well as preventing unnecessary evaporation, watering in the cool of the evening (or early morning) promotes the best grass growth. Even better is to water late at night; during the summer grass grows more at night than during the day so it can make best use of the water at this time.

3) Avoid over-watering! A dry spell can tempt us into unnecessary watering, but even the most precisely-controlled irrigation system won't give you the necessary control. Too much water will force the air out of the soil, causing problems for the microbes essential to healthy root feeding and development.

Watering newly seeded or turfed lawns

If you've just invested time and money in creating some new lawn, you *will* need to do some extra watering.

Newly seeded

Water is one of the essential catalysts for seed germination. Most seeds will germinate within only a few days if watered correctly, but this means watering *as often as it takes* to keep the top few millimetres of the soil permanently moist. Just watering in the mornings and evenings may allow it to dry out too much in the warm weather, delaying or preventing germination. As a rule of thumb, one square metre of newly seeded ground only requires 10-15 seconds of water to keep the seed moist. Do this as often as the weather dictates and you will see much better germination than by simply leaving the sprinkler on for hour after hour! Then, when it has grown into a little seedling, don't neglect it! Avoid the hot daytime sun but be sure to make sure it doesn't get too thirsty.

Newly turfed

To give your beautiful new turf the best chances, you must water it carefully. This begins before it is laid by watering the soil to create a moist base for the turf. Then as soon as it is laid, another watering is necessary. Finally, water well and deep for at least one week after laying. The aim is to activate the roots and send them down into the moist soil. You will know when this is achieved - when you carefully try to lift the turf, it won't budge! In moderate weather you can expect to reduce watering after a week, but even then monitor the weather and be ready to give it a good drink in dry conditions.

discussion

Q: Can I water too much?

Yes, and many people do, especially if they have an automated watering system. Firstly, watering can be a knee-jerk response to the lawn looking half-dead. There may be other reasons for this - lack of nutrients, problems in the thatch, cutting too short and so on. In these cases, the problem will continue when the rains return, so watering is wasteful and not much real help at all.

Remember what I said earlier about the average rainfall? Well, if you leap out to water every time it's dry you will seriously risk what I call 'stagnant pond syndrome' - a black, stagnant layer in the soil. The only lawns that can cope with a daily drenching are the professionally maintained lawns with good drainage and soil conditions.

Q: Can I water too little?

If you are going to water the lawn, make it a good watering because, yes, watering too lightly will just encourage shallow rooting, and can even drive the roots upwards in search of the water that is insufficient to filter through to the soil.

Q: I have an automatic sprinkler system, how much should I water?

Start off with small amounts, but regularly (or you risk under-watering - see above). Monitor the lawn closely - you're looking for signs that the water is not draining through OR that small patches appear to be drying very quickly. And don't automatically switch it on at the same time each day - check it is needed, be observant and frugal. Your lawn (and the planet) will thank you for it!

Q: How often should I water?

No one can tell you categorically how often as every lawn is different - you must simply monitor the conditions day by day. When it's very hot, you may need to water each day to ensure it gets the right amount of soaking. In cooler but dry conditions, it may just be a weekly job.

Q: I'm happy to leave my grass a little brown in the summer, but should I mow it when it's like this?

Unless you're in the middle of a huge drought, the brown will represent only some of the grass types in your lawn; the others, like dwarf ryegrasses, will be doing just fine. So, yes, you will still need to cut. However, try raising the cutting height one or two notches to reduce the stress on the plants. Also, keep the blade really sharp for a good, clean cut. You can even sprinkle the clippings back on the lawn to add a little more protection, food and even water!

"You may think I am a water conservationist. Maybe, maybe not – I just believe passionately in working WITH rather than against nature. You'll always hear people say "Oh, don't worry – it'll come back to life!" – and they're right. Be prepared to lose a bit of colour in mid-summer – a healthy plant should be allowed to shut down – think of it as a summer siesta! If you look after its environment, the lawn will come back to its green glory when the conditions are right".

additional techniques
laying new turf

INCLUDES: Underlying reasons for needing to returf; planning the new lawn; preparing the ground; laying the turf

Laying a new lawn with turf can be exciting, offering all kinds of creative opportunities. It can also be expensive and a terrible mistake if you don't do your homework first! So, before you order and lay your turf, invest a little time in analysing what may have gone wrong with the old lawn – and why. This will give your newly turfed lawn not just a good start in life, but a long life too. And if you are creating a brand new lawn on a fresh site, you still need good preparation which includes identifying potential problems for the future.

Underlying reasons for needing to returf

The most important lesson in creating a new lawn is to implement the same thorough maintenance programme you would for an older lawn. Healthy new turf will very quickly turn into poor lawn if previous problems or lack of maintenance are allowed to continue. So, if you are replacing an old, worn out or struggling lawn, the same underlying reasons for its poor condition will or can eventually affect the new turf. Diagnose these problems and apply the correct solution, and you can look forward to a thriving and healthy lawn.

Let's look at the most common reasons why an established lawn might have failed – and what you can do *before* laying the new turf.

Lack of maintenance

This is the most obvious reason and, if you have just moved into a new home and inherited the garden, it's not your fault! But you can still use the condition of the lawn as a timely reminder that good routine maintenance is essential on all lawns, new and old alike.

Remedy

You have already begun to put things right by using this book! Study the 12-month programme section and begin planning your routine maintenance.

Poor soil

While there is not much we can do to change our soil, it is often overlooked as a vital component of the lawn. There *are* some ways to maintain good soil health, and ignoring these could be the reason for the failed lawn you are about to replace.

Remedy

Start by reading the chapter on soil (p52). You can do an easy soil test to see what pH you have. Sand can be useful for improving the surface soil quality. And remember - once the turf is down, it's down! This is the one chance you have to prepare the entire soil bed for years of strong grass support.

Poor drainage

Soil is often blamed for poor drainage, but there are often other causes, ones which are easier to rectify. Aeration (p64) is a 'must', but you may also find that patios or paths are channelling excess water onto the grass or preventing it from draining freely. Many gardens have been hard-landscaped in recent years, with concrete structures causing water-flow problems.

Remedy

First, study the lawn and surrounding area carefully, particularly during and after rainfall. Also examine the condition of the thatch (p40), as this may be the underlying cause. And be prepared to alter the fall of the lawn or add drainage channels for pathways and other structures.

Shade

Read the section on shade (p192) - it will help you understand the extent of the problem and whether you can reduce it or not. Then observe the existing lawn at different times of day to assess the amount of shade. You may be surprised to discover how little shade is cast, in which case maybe shade is not the villain after all!

Remedy

If you don't want to cut down the offending trees or shrubs, think about changing the design of the new lawn to avoid these areas. Or perhaps the tree has simply never been pruned and can be better controlled in the future? It is also worth speaking to a good turf supplier to see if they can recommend a suitable grass mix.

Planning the new lawn

Before ordering your turf you need to plan the layout of the lawn, and this is a great opportunity to alleviate long-standing problems.

Mowing

The most important goal in planning is easy and effective mowing. Revisit the chapter on mowing (p78) and remind yourself about corners and turning areas. Some careful thought now can save you a lot of time and effort when mowing the lawn!

Trees and shade

Don't just look at the existing trees and shrubs - think what additions you may like in the future! And try to design your lawn shape to avoid unnecessary dark areas.

Preparing the ground

Reducing soil compaction

If you can, now is the time to widen any narrow paths or walkways. Narrow paths (see Problem Areas, p187) concentrate normal footfall onto small, vulnerable parts of the lawn, resulting in soil compaction and increased wear and tear. Simply by widening them, or even rethinking the shape or contour, you can reduce this damaging effect.

Bumps, slopes and levels

This is also the best time to sort out any unwanted unevenness or improve existing slopes. You may even want to alter the level of the lawn. So, plan this carefully, remembering to factor in the extra soil you might need (your turf supplier may be able to supply this). You can read more about levelling on p196.

And now you're ready...

... well, almost. Before you can lay your turf **you need to buy it**! This needs some research - compare suppliers, talk to them about which turf mixture they suggest, ask about soil if you're changing ground levels - and of course, measure the area carefully (your supplier will give you help to do this).

Finally, you need to plan for **post-delivery turf care**. The turf will be freshly dug (usually on the day of delivery) but soon warms up and begins to deteriorate - certainly faster than you can lay it! So it's best to be ready to unroll it, even if you can't lay it straightaway. This lets it breathe and is easy to water if necessary (never water it when rolled up as this will speed up the deterioration).

Here are some simple Dos and Don'ts:

- Don't cut corners when preparing the project; good preparation prevents expensive mistakes.

- Do prepare for good watering.

- Do lay your turf as soon as possible before it begins losing its colour.

- Don't lay new turf over old. Remove all existing vegetation and then work over the ground to remove compaction in the soil.

- Do plan from the start for your routine maintenance. Keep the lawn looking as good as it does when the turf first beds in.

discussion.

General

Q: Can I lay turf at any time of the year?

Yes, you can, except when there is snow or frost on the ground. Just remember to prepare carefully for the necessary maintenance, bearing in mind the seasonal conditions.

Q: Can I use different types of turf for different areas in the garden (e.g. a shady spot)?

Yes, you can, although you may have to hunt around different suppliers to find the right grass mixtures. It is still not a guarantee that you will solve any problems through this alone, and of course having different mixtures may show up noticeably in the garden.

When new turf is delivered

Q: How long can my turf sit on the pallet before I have to unload?

Turf is a great conductor of heat and quickly stresses if left on the pallet - more so if still rolled up. You should aim to be unrolling it and laying it immediately if you can - and if not, think in terms of hours rather than days - so prepare well!

What to do after laying

Q: How long will it take to bed in and 'root' properly?

As always, you will have to go out and assess this yourself by checking the root system. If the turf cannot be lifted then it has bedded in. There is no timescale on this, but be aware that once it has bedded in, you still need to care for ongoing root development and health.

Q: How soon can I mow new turf?

Before mowing, check that the turf has knitted (firmly rooted into the soil) and make sure your lawn mower blade is sharp! See the mowing section (p78) about how much grass to remove.

Q: How soon do I need to scarify or aerate my new turf?

Once your new turf has bedded in and is looking great, this may be the last thing on your mind. However, you're right to ask - my suggestion would be to aerate any time from six months after the lawn has been laid, to fit with your aeration schedule. Allowing oxygen into any lawn is very important so don't leave it too long before you aerate (8-12 months maximum).

Q: How soon should I feed my new lawn?

If you have managed to apply a pre-turfing fertiliser, then this should be absorbed by the roots during the first 6-8 weeks. After this, keep an eye on the new lawn and refer to the chapter on Nutrition (p90). Your reputable turf supplier will also help with any advice on suitable fertilisers.

Q: Why do mushrooms appear soon after my lawn has been laid?

These are the fruiting body of the fungi *Basidiomycetes*. The vegetative part of the fungi lives in the soil, feeding on plant materials. When preparing your soil for its new turf, you disturb organic debris. The spores are then brought to life and in warm, moist conditions you will get a flush of toadstools. They are not dangerous (although I do not advise eating them). Just mow them or brush them off. As your lawn grows and you begin aerating, the bacteria in the soil will soon balance out the ecosystem beneath the surface and you should rarely see them again.

Watering

Q: How should I water new turf?

Watering turf is the important final step that you must plan for in advance, ensuring you have a good water supply and enough time! Make sure you have a good quality sprinkler and hosepipe (before your turf arrives) and that pressure is good, especially if you have a large lawn. Do not flood the turf but ensure soils become and remain moist, otherwise you could cause shallow rooting. Your turf supplier can give you some useful watering advice.

Q: When should I water?

For optimum results, water very early in the morning or late at night. Evenings are better as the water has a longer time to absorb into the soil profile and the plant has more chance to use the water. However, daytime can be useful (or indeed necessary in very dry periods) especially if the sunshine is not too strong.

Q: If it rains, should I still water?

If your new lawn still needs good watering, a quick rain shower may or may not be enough. You are the one who must monitor it and see. You can peel back a corner of turf to see if it has rained enough to penetrate the soil. However, even if you don't need to water that day, use a water butt to capture the rain for another time as it can give much better results than tap water.

Q: How long do I need to keep watering?

Every lawn is different but 2-3 months is usually enough time. Monitor the new lawn carefully, looking for signs that it is surviving on drier days.

Some other dos and don'ts

- Do NOT lay turf onto an existing lawn. Prepare the soil properly and carefully - you only get one chance to do this!

- DO use pre-turfing fertiliser. It will aid the roots when they start to develop and ensure the turf 'knits' more strongly.

- DO buy slightly more turf than you need. There is nothing worse than not being able to finish the job because you have been left a few rolls short. It is usually cheaper to over-buy the first time than to pay for a top-up order.

- Do NOT buy very cheap turf. If you see turf at a very special price, be suspicious; if it seems too good to be true, it probably is.

- Do NOT water the turf when it is on the pallet. If you cannot lay on the day it arrives, take the turf off the pallet and stack carefully, unrolled, in a shady, well ventilated area. You can then water it.

- Whenever possible, buy direct from the grower or use a recommended distributor - they are the experts. If you have to buy from garden centres or DIY merchants, pick up the turf, inspect it and even smell it. You never know how long it has been sitting there for!

additional techniques
top dressing

INCLUDES: What is top dressing? Do I need it? What to buy; how to apply it; what can go wrong

Originally emanating from the golf and sports industry, top dressing is nowadays often talked about with regard to domestic lawns. However, as with other interventions adapted from the non-domestic sector, we should consider top dressing within the broader context of good lawn care (making sure we're not overlooking an easier or more necessary remedy) and then decide when, or if, it is really necessary. Yes, top dressings can help in a number of situations such as thatch control and seed germination. But it can also be very expensive and of little meaningful benefit. This short chapter, posing and answering the common questions, will help you to make your own decision.

What is top dressing?

Top dressing is simply material that is added to turf in a shallow layer to correct surface irregularities, aid thatch control, enhance seed germination and improve soil structures. In the UK there are no standards governing top dressing. This explains why the bag of top dressing you buy might contain anything from a high quality turf dressing (graded sand and loam/soil) to nothing more than sifted soil or even sand which can still look enticingly crumbled in a well-presented bag. However, whilst most dressings work to some extent - improving levels, thatch and soil - is it sensible to throw any old thing down without knowing exactly what it is?

Do I need it?

If you have a very fine lawn and you use a cylinder mower then yes, you do need to top dress. Your fine lawn and the design of your mower demand smooth, even surfaces. A regular top dressing programme is an essential part of maintaining this (see 'What do I buy and where?' below).

However, if you use a rotary mower and are happy with the results you are getting from your lawn programme, you won't be chasing the perfect billiard table finish. And because you will rarely be cutting lower than 25mm, your mower will cope perfectly well with small surface irregularities. If you have isolated patches that need levelling, you can try different methods (see 'Levelling' p196)

So, with dressings that may not do very much and lawns which may not need it anyway, top dressing can sometimes just be an expensive distraction with little real benefit. To help you decide for your own lawn, let's cross-examine some of the most common reasons given for using a top dressing.

1. **Thatch control:** a common reason, but before you decide to top dress have you given enough attention to your scarification programme?

2. **Improving a poor clay soil:** if you are hoping to build up a layer above the existing soil, the amount of dressing you need will make this a thankless and expensive task! Have you really done all you can to improve grass growth? Why not revisit 'Your Lawn in 3-D' and the 'Techniques' sections first?

3. **Correcting levels after too much hollow-tining:** here there is justification in using a good quality top dressing to even out the surface. You will probably need a mixture with a high soil content.

4. **Aiding seed germination:** people are quick to cite this reason, and a top dressing of pure sand certainly looks very professional. But remember, sand is inert and hence of little use to the seeds. So, if you do want to top dress before sowing, use a loam/sand mix and only to a depth of one or two millimetres.

5. **Everyone else seems to be doing it:** so what? Your lawn programme combines proven interventions with your own informed judgement based on observation and testing. Don't do something just because it's fashionable!

What do I buy and where?

What to buy depends on your type of mower.

If you use a **cylinder mower** in order to get fantastic results, you must get fantastic top dressing for your lawn. The supplier must be able to show you a specification sheet detailing exactly what is in the dressing - the proportion and quality of sand, particle shape and size, and the loam or soil content. Use a mix with a higher sand content (say 70%) if you are top dressing the entire lawn; and for levelling small areas, use anything from 70%-100% soil dressing. However, a specialist supplier will always be able to advise you.

With **rotary mowing** and a standard lawn in good condition, the actual quality of dressing is not so important - it's how you apply it that matters (see p134).

Where to buy: I would always recommend going to a reputable supplier as buying cheap usually means it is of poor rather than adequate quality. Always explain to the supplier that you need top dressing for an *existing* lawn - make it clear you are not creating a lawn from scratch. This means that a general purpose dressing should be fine, but still ask to see a specification sheet.

How do I apply it?

How much and how often?

A regular top dressing programme won't be cheap and is labour-intensive. However, little and often is the best approach for the following reason:

- A light dressing (between 1 and 5mm) can be done with more ease and speed

- Light dressings won't leave you with brownish appearance for a long period of time

- Grass growth is stunted less by a light dressing and mowing can resume much sooner

- A light dressing won't interfere so much with your normal lawn care routines

- You don't have to store as much material on site.

As for regularity, a rough guide for a croquet lawn finish is anything between two and six dressings per year, but I recommend starting at two and seeing how it goes. If you can only top dress once or twice and need to apply it more thickly, never do this in winter (November-February) as the grass must be growing well and be able to push through the dressing.

What can go wrong?

Something can always go wrong, so be prepared:

1) **Choose the best product available** (within the mixture range you are looking for). Talk to reputable suppliers (and generally avoid builders as their material is usually sharp sand for building patios and walls, not a turf dressing). A poor quality product can affect grass growth.

2) **Fit it around your lawn programme**. Based on the reason for doing it, work out how many applications you need and co-ordinate it with your lawn programme so that it isn't disrupted. For example, don't top dress a few weeks before you scarify. And if top dressing for thatch control, finish other thatch control procedures like scarification first so that the dressing can get into the lower profile of the thatch.

3) **Choose the right soil and lawn conditions**. Don't apply dressing to frozen or wet soils as this can spread any disease you may have in the lawn. And if the grass is under stress, top dressing will simply add to this, so rectify it first or wait for conditions to improve.

discussion

Q: When should I top dress?
As a rule of thumb it should be done when grass growth is healthy, between March and October. You also need to decide how many applications you intend during the year and plan these around any other lawn operations.

Q: Does it matter if the weather is dry or wet when I top dress?
This is definitely a dry day job, although being able to predict some rainfall for when you have finished is good, especially where seed has been added.

Q: Is it OK to walk across the lawn straight after dressing?
Yes it is, unless you have sown some seed into the dressing.

Q: How soon can I mow after applying a top dressing?
The main consideration is how quickly the grass regains its normal growth rate (the top dressing will initially stunt growth). If you are cylinder mowing and you add water after the dressing to help it 'bed in', you can resume mowing more quickly. If you're using a rotary mower, the grass will be that little bit longer anyway and so growth resumes more easily.

In both cases, however, you must expect some of the top dressing to interfere with the blade, so be ready to sharpen it soon after you resume cutting (another reason not to rush into cylinder mowing!).

Q: Do I need to water a newly applied dressing?
Watering after top dressing is always a good idea - but rainfall is more effective than a hose or sprinkler. The benefit of water is that it reduces the stress on the grass and helps it to grow through the dressing more quickly.

Q: Should I feed before or afterwards?
As you are aiming to top dress when grass growth is already good and strong it is unlikely you will want to feed in the same period. If for some reason you do, both before and after are fine.

Q: Do I need to level it out?

This depends on how heavily and how evenly it has been applied. If you are concerned, give it time for the dressing to dry out first and then a light blower, a broom or even the back of a rake can be used to level it out.

Q: What about aerating first and brushing down the holes?

This has been a common instruction for many years as it can improve drainage, but I question its necessity in the domestic lawn. In professional lawn care (golf courses etc) this is generally done using a hollow-tine aeration and is referred to as 'soil exchange'. But remember, these are lawns which need to remain green and open all year round for business reasons! With the domestic lawn, putting a sandy substance down a hollow-tine hole sounds good in principle but it is hard to do with any consistency or accuracy. If you want to improve your drainage, why not simply add an extra aeration to your annual programme?

additional techniques
overseeding

Even the best-kept grass will die eventually – through old age, extreme weather or a mixture or both. And so there are times when we need to introduce new grass into the lawn by overseeding. It's also a way to balance out the species in the lawn, although there is probably a good reason why the dominant species likes your lawn so much! Overseeding is a simple concept but the results can be a little unreliable. Often the reseeding operation is necessary because the lawn is under some kind of stress, so it is a delicate process. However, with a little preparation and some pre- and post-germination care, you can achieve some good results this way.

Preparation

Before embarking on overseeding, we need to realise that we're going to be setting up a competition in the lawn for water, food and even sunlight. Each of these is necessary for successful germination and to help the young plants establish themselves, but they are also in high demand from the existing grasses in your lawn. And the bottom line is that these adult plants are going to win the battle if you don't give the seeds some help.

For an entire lawn reseeding operation, do the following:

1. Start your preparation by mowing, and mowing lower than you normally would. This will remove as much of the leaf blade as it's safe to do, allowing sunlight to penetrate into the sward and onto the seed bed. This will initially leave the grass struggling a little, but the feed and watering you give to the newly germinated seedlings will help it to recover.

2. Scarify heavily - and aerate too. Scarifying will reduce the thatch levels and increase contact with the soil ready for sowing the seed, while aerating creates nice new holes ready for the seedlings' roots to work down into.

3. Having scarified, instead of removing the cores from the surface, raise the height of the scarifier to just above ground level and let the scarifier grind them up, returning the rich bacteria to the soil. Then spread the seed and finally lightly pull the loose core-soil around until evenly distributed.

4. As an alternative to 3 (or in addition), you can completely top dress the lawn with a suitable top dressing to aid quicker germination.

If you are simply reseeding a small area, follow the same procedure but do it all with hand tools.

During and after germination

TIP: Some experienced gardeners like to apply mycorrhizae (a fungus) when overseeding. It creates a mutual relationship with the new grass plants by attaching or growing inside the roots. This hugely extends the roots' capacity to absorb water and mineral nutrients.

First, be aware that you will almost never achieve 100% success; 70% would be regarded as a very satisfactory germination rate when overseeding. It also helps to use similar cultivars to those that are already growing well in the lawn - they clearly like it there while other species may not thrive quite as well.

Watering: once the seed is down, water is vital to swell the seed until it germinates and pops into life. So you must water regularly if the weather is dry. You don't need the water to penetrate deep into the soil as the seed can't reach it there, so just keep the first couple of millimetres moist. If it begins to dry out, germination will simply take longer.

Feeding: when the seeds germinate, apply a high phosphate food (eg 6-18-6) as soon as you can. This will feed the new seedlings and help them develop strong, thick leaf blades quickly.

Mowing: finally, adjust your mowing for a few months. Always keep the blade sharp (which you should do anyway) but mow slightly higher than usual. This gives the new plants the chance to grow stronger and longer, ready to cope with all the stresses that a modern lawn can face.

Routine scarification also creates a convenient seed bed!

common problems

Contents:

plus ADDITIONAL PROBLEMS:

weed control

INCLUDES: What is a weed? What to do if weeds are taking over; how weed killer works; how it is applied; what to do afterwards

In days gone by we were happy to throw chemicals at our gardens to eradicate anything that we didn't want there, regardless of the impact on other organisms and the general eco-balance. Nowadays we're far better informed about the dangers of this recklessness - and in any case, many of the harmful chemicals are no longer available to the domestic market. But is it always wrong to resort to chemical weed killers?

The best way to control weeds is to prevent them - and that comes down to good lawn care. It's true! The healthy lawn simply doesn't leave enough space for weeds to become a problem. Today's garden chemicals, however, don't actually deserve the bad reputation they have. They are much less toxic than in the past and have been continually developed to work efficiently without adverse impact on anything else.

"I once ran a US-designed and maintained golf course with the best quality grass of any in Europe. People assumed we must be drenching the grass in chemicals to keep it so good, but not at all! During a talk at a local college, I laid out a complete season's collection of empty pesticide containers - it didn't even cover the table top, and this was for a 260 acre site! And the reason why? By concentrating instead on good, sensible maintenance we simply didn't have a significant weed problem".

What is a weed?

As with any other part of the garden, a weed is simply a plant in the wrong place. Lawn weeds such as dandelions, daisies and clover are perfectly attractive little plants but not what most gardeners want in their lawns. However, you only really find serious weed problems in badly neglected lawns. Indeed you can have a fantastic looking lawn with a few inconspicuous and harmless weeds nestling amongst the grass!

No room for a serious weed problem!

The common weeds include:

Dandelion

Daisy

Clover

Speedwell

Selfheal

Yarrow

Thistle

Chickweed

Lesser Trefoil

Plantain

Hawkbit

Cat's Ear

Field Woodrush

What to do if weeds are taking over

The best type of weed control is healthy grass but if you *do* need to intervene, your choice is either hand weeding or chemical spraying. For hand weeding, you can buy cleverly designed and inexpensive hand tools for extracting stubborn dandelions - these ensure you remove the entire tap root, not just the surface plant. Then just use a mix of soil and seed to repair the hole.

However, if your lawn looks like the picture above you need to apply a spray treatment. Before you do, there are a few things you need to know.

How weed killer works

Today, most weed killers are essentially growth hormones. They work by accelerating the rate of the plant's growth until it exhausts itself and dies.

How it is applied

Applying weed killer to a large lawn area is tricky and it is best to hire professional help. Here's why:

- Professionals have access to better chemical treatments

- Effective use of the equipment is a skilled job

- Judging how much chemical to apply requires expertise.

What to do after treating with weed killer

The best thing you can do afterwards is to improve your lawn maintenance programme. Get the grass and its environment healthy and you should be able to keep the problem well under control.

The great 'Feed 'n' Weed' debate

There are opposing views in the lawn world about the widely-available 'feed 'n' weed' products and their use. Personally, I am against any indiscriminate or poorly informed use of garden chemicals. I prefer a balanced approach to gardening which, as much as possible, maintains a healthy and natural ecosystem within the garden. But the key question is whether these products are effective.

However alluring the packaging, 'feed 'n' weed' products are indiscriminate tools. They apply weedkiller 'willy-nilly' whether it is needed or not, and with risk to the soil below. For isolated patches of weeds why not use a spot-treatment? You have far more control and use far fewer chemicals. And if you think the problem is too big for that, do consider consulting a reputable lawn professional who can extend the spot-approach to a larger area.

discussion

Q: How should I handle and store garden chemicals?

From reading this chapter you'll know I think that these chemicals should not be on general sale. However, if you do use them, always wear protective gloves when handling! Keep them safely locked away and out of reach of children and animals (pets and wild). And please don't disposeof them down drains (see below). Look on the label too - they have a finite shelf life and lose their efficacy over time.

Q: I have an old bottle of weed killer in the shed. How do I dispose of it safely?

As with anything remotely toxic or dangerous, take the bottle to your local refuse centre - they'll know how to dispose of it safely.

Q: Is there a method that is more accurate (and less random) than spraying?

Yes - you can buy little weed control sticks made of wax, and spot-treatment devices for hitting individual plants. And of course, you can just dig them out!

Q: I don't use chemicals, but my neighbour sprays his lawn. Will this affect mine?

Unless it is very windy you'll be fine. However the chemicals work on contact and so your neighbour should be striving to make sure none of the expensive chemical escapes into the surrounding garden space.

Q: When is the best time to use weed killer?

The weed killer accelerates growth until the plant can't cope any more and dies. So, obviously, you need to use it when the weeds are actively growing. But many weeds germinate all year round, so there isn't a 'best' time of the year and you may find you need more than one application.

Q: **How safe is it for pets and children?**

Direct contact should always be avoided. However, once the weed killer has been absorbed by the plant's leaves (usually 1-2 hours) the main danger has passed. Better still, however, to use targeted spot treatment.

Q: **Why do weeds appear after I have applied a weedkiller?**

You're seeing the newly germinated weeds suddenly growing very fast - it's the way that the chemicals kill them.

Q: **It says on my bottle; apply 20ml in 10 litres of water. Is this correct?**

Spraying is a very imprecise activity - nozzles come in different sizes and sprayers empty at different rates. So, this type of instruction is only very approximate.

Q: **Should I apply weed killer through a watering can?**

No. Even with a very fine rose the rate of water flow is too great, washing much of the killer off the leaves.

moss

INCLUDES: Causes; removal (plus extra discussion points on moss control and moss killer)

Some like it, many loathe it – but the bottom line is that moss competes with other plants in its environment, especially grass. So, whether you want a traditional grass lawn or something more contemporary (wild flower meadow, chamomile, etc), moss is not your best friend. Yes, you may hear some TV gardeners talk keenly about the bouncy spring and visual interest it adds to the lawn but they fail to mention the tremendous work you'll be creating for yourself if you encourage moss! As it gets a foothold, moss thins out your grass; and the thinner your grass, the more space for the encroaching moss – until all you've got is moss – no lawn left at all. But there's more; even if you do like moss, even if you are prepared to tolerate a little of it, you need to understand why it's there – because moss is a sure sign that something is fundamentally wrong with your lawn, something this chapter will help you to diagnose.

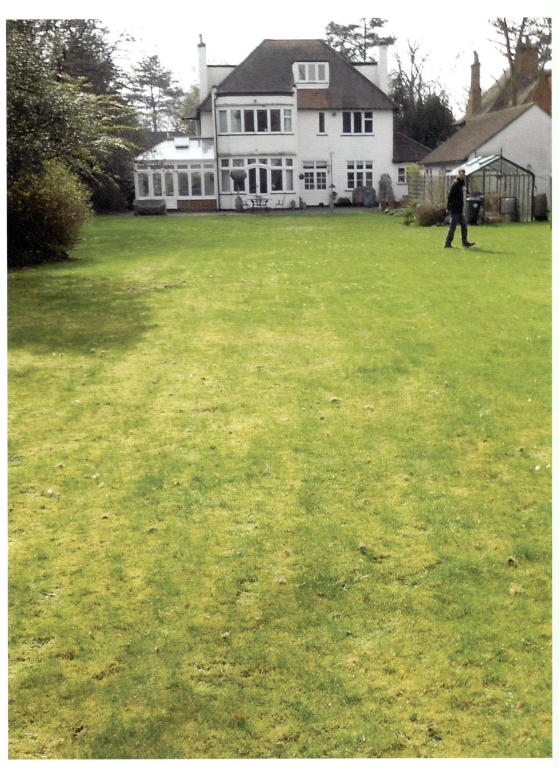

As you can see here, shade is NOT always the villain
when it comes to a moss invasion!

Causes - what can moss tell you about your lawn's health?

Moss grows in tightly clumped mats, and because it thrives on moisture-retentive surface, it loves growing in lawns! There is plenty you can do to minimise this unwanted imposter once you have worked out why it is there in the first place. And this will almost always relate to one or more of these - drainage, nutrition, shade, thatch and mowing. So let's first look at how each of these common lawn problems encourage moss.

1. Drainage

If you see puddles of surface water collecting and not draining away, it can indicate a problem. And, with our changing and unpredictable weather, we face more flash flooding and prolonged rainfall, making drainage even more of a priority.

Fortunately the solution already lies within your annual lawn care programme - routine aeration and scarification. Both of these will help maintain a controlled and healthy thatch layer, essential for good surface drainage. Correct nutrition and ensuring you mow at the correct height (not too short) will also help. Each of these is explained further below.

2. Nutrition

How you feed your lawn - or how you don't - will impact on your moss problem, but not necessarily because moss is competing directly with the grass for nutrients. It actually relates to the thatch layer (and the resulting moisture retention on the lawn surface).

As with other aspects of your yearly lawn care programme, get the nutrition right (see Nutrition, p90) and you should see a reduction or even eradication of your moss problem.

Here, scarification revealed the true cause of the moss - poor nutrition. An urgent feed is now needed.

3. Shade

It is true that lawns and shade don't go well together, but we often blame shade unfairly for all kinds of problems. And moss is a great example of this. If you have a shady area with thinly growing grass then of course moss might take a hold, especially if the shady area is moist. But before you go chopping down the offending tree or bush, take a closer look. The problem - and the solution - may lie with moisture, air flow, nutrients or grass species, all things which relate to the tree's presence *and* which can be improved without felling it.

Problem Areas (p187) explains the implications of shady areas and provides excellent methods for improving the grass without resorting to unnecessary landscaping.

Excess thatch brought out by scarifying

4. Thatch

Well-managed thatch is an essential part of the lawn structure, but its relationship to moss is simple - dense and thick thatch prevents good surface drainage, holding onto the moisture which moss craves. So, the answer is 'simple' - make thatch management a central part of your yearly programme and you will minimise the moss problem.

Thatch (p40) signposts you to all the advice you need to manage your crucial thatch layer.

5. Mowing

Mowing isn't just necessary for good aesthetic results; it is a key process in maintaining a healthy sward. Cutting to the right height (see Mowing p78) is crucial to good lawn health because of its impact on thatch, drainage and nutrition. So how does this relate to moss?

Generally speaking, cutting too short will encourage moss growth - the grass cannot thrive and the sun will be able to reach the soil and can bake it dry, preventing good surface drainage. Both of these symptoms give moss a chance to take hold. Of course, keep cutting it too short and eventually even the moss can't thrive - but then you'll have no lawn either!

Removing moss from the lawn

Both photos show how using moss killer without scarifying first will not kill the entire plant

Scarification

The simplest way to remove moss is to scarify the lawn (See 'Scarification' p98). And remember - you're really just gently teasing the moss from the surface - it doesn't have long roots so there is no need to penetrate the turf too deeply.

Moss killer

Moss killer (ferrous sulphate) works best as a liquid application (administered using a sprayer or watering can). If applied in granular form or as part of a 'feed, weed and moss killer' application, it is impossible for it to attach itself effectively to every moss plant.

So, mixed correctly with large volumes of water, moss killer will not just reach more moss plants but will kill them without the blackening effect too - and without the grass suffering either. If it does blacken, it simply means that you have used too much of the moss killer with insufficient water, leading to the scorching or burning effect.

Here you can see the more effective outcome of moss killer applied AFTER scarifying

Combining scarification with use of moss killer

In the past we were advised to kill the moss first before scarifying, and then simply rake it out. However, this is wrong - for two reasons. Firstly, if you apply killer *before* scarifying and then inspect the blackening, dying moss, you will probably notice healthy green parts at the base of the plants. The moss is not fully dead and can easily recover. So, scarify first in order to thin out the thatch and moss. When you then apply the killer it has a much better chance of reaching these lower parts of the plant. Secondly, moss spreads by spores, invisible to the human eye. If you apply moss killer first but some of these survive, scarifying simply scatters them, helping the moss to spread. This is why I always recommend applying moss killer *after* every scarification.

Never give up!

You shouldn't become obsessed but it is best to assume that moss will always be trying to take hold when the conditions are right. To stay on top of it, use moss products during the winter to help control the spread of spores. Beyond this, prevention and cure come down to good lawn management, avoiding as much as possible the related lawn problems described above.

discussion

1: About Moss

Q: How does moss get into my lawn?
Moss plants develop from spores blown in the wind and bedding into the thatch - and these are invisible to the naked eye.

Q: So how will I know if I have spores in my thatch?
You won't. That's why a good maintenance programme is so important, helping to keep the moss at bay by avoiding the conditions that encourage growth.

Q: When does moss most frequently invade?
From September to March can be the worst months, although with more extreme weather patterns, conditions suitable for new moss can occur throughout the year (especially if it creates problems with thatch or makes regular mowing difficult).

This lawn took about two weeks to recover from scarifying and moss killing

2: About Moss Control

Q: Is there one single intervention I MUST do to control moss?

I wish it was that easy, but no! It's a combination of everything needed to maintain healthy grass - scarifying, aeration, correct mowing, drainage, nutrition - and moss killer.

Q: Can't I just apply moss killer each year?

Prevention is better than cure and yes, you'll find plenty of products labelled 'moss killer'. They certainly help and you should use them from time to time routinely alongside your nutrition programme. But remember, simply applying moss killer risks ignoring other underlying causes such as mowing, thatch and surface drainage.

Q: When I'm scarifying, should I try to remove ALL the moss plants?

The answer is actually "no". Of course you want to remove as much moss as possible but it must not be at the expense of the grass. Scarify too aggressively and you risk thinning out the grass too much which creates inviting new space for new moss to establish.

Q: Is it true than I can make moss worse by scarifying without using a moss killer?

Yes! Scarifying by itself can help the active moss spores to spread around the lawn and establish new colonies.

Q: What should I do with the moss that I remove from the lawn?

You could just burn it or throw it away, but why not try recycling it? By itself it is not ideal for compost but you can try mixing it with grass cuttings and general garden waste. Or you could give it to friends for lining their hanging baskets!

discussion

3: About Moss Killer

Q: Should I scarify before or after applying moss killer?

If you use moss killer before scarifying, you will kill the top part of the plant but not the bottom part. So always scarify *before* using moss killer. This opens up the sward to allow much better penetration and performance of the liquid moss killer.

Q: What it the best time of year to use a moss killer?

It's a good idea to apply moss killer in winter even if you don't have any visible moss as it can appear very quickly during the wet winter months. Do it at the same time as your winter feed, but remember that a liquid application works far better than a granular one, and do scarify before using it.

Q: Should I apply a moss killer even if I do not have moss?

Yes, as this helps prevent it from taking hold. Applications during winter are good as well as after scarification.

Q: Is a moss killer in a bag of 'feed, weed and moss killer' suitable to use?

Yes it is, but combining two or three things in one application often lessens the chance of any of them working correctly. Products work best when you have a single product for a single purpose. Also, moss killer works far better in liquid form when it can reach all of the plant.

Q: When I have applied moss killer before, everything goes black and burns, even the grass. What am I doing wrong?

This is probably down to one of two problems. Either you are using it in non-liquid (granular) form, making it hard to achieve an even spread and letting it instead concentrate in particular areas, or you are simply using too much! Use liquid killer, at the right concentration, and always check the product carefully for application information.

Ferrous Sulphate

Q: How do I apply liquid moss killer?

You can use a watering can but this is slow, laborious and inaccurate. Knapsacks sprayers or 'push along' sprayers are better but even with these it can be hard to achieve and maintain the ideal application rate. Getting it right is a skilled job, so if you are in any doubt, call in an expert first!

Q: Are there any organic alternatives to mainstream chemical moss killers?

Yes there are but none can replace entirely the best environmental approach – a good lawn care programme!

common diseases

INCLUDES: Red thread; fusarium; rust; mildew; other less common diseases

In the domestic garden, lawn disease is a sign that the lawn is under stress – cut too short, lacking in nutrition (or maybe too much nutrition!) or victim to changing weather patterns. The spores of our common diseases lie dormant in all lawns and when the lawn becomes weak and conditions are right, they strike. However, diseases are not actually very common, although our changing weather patterns – the same rain as before but in heavier, shorter bursts, and drought lasting for longer periods – are putting lawns under greater stress. Also it is getting much harder to buy turf fungicides and other chemical treatments. So as well as maintaining a balanced lawn care programme, it pays to be on the lookout for the most common diseases.

A particular problem for the domestic gardener is that advice often comes from turf experts who look after golf courses and sports fields. Being large and exposed, these are typically windier, cooler and drier than the average lawn and benefit from regular dew removal and purpose-built drainage. So the techniques used there may not necessarily work in the domestic garden environment.

The principal villains

So, who are the chief villains? Well, there are two principals - red thread and fusarium - and two runners-up - rust and powdery mildew. None is a common sight but each can blight the appearance of the lawn or undermine its health, so it pays to understand how each can take hold - and what you can do to treat it. However, the best treatment is to look after your lawn. As with humans, the healthier it is, the more able it is to fight any disease itself.

Red Thread

Our most common domestic lawn disease, red thread was rarely seen in the past (or at least rarely noticed) and was easily halted by changing weather conditions or a quick nitrogen feed. You might have spotted it from May or June onwards but then by September it had disappeared. And because it only affects the leaf part and not the whole plant, recovery was quick. However, we are beginning to see it more often thanks to changing weather patterns.

What is red thread?

Caused by the corticioid fungus *Laetisaria fuciformis*, red thread is a fungal infection which attacks the grass in two stages. The first produces the thin red strands on leaf blades which give it its name. These are germinated stromata which can have been lying in the soil for years. The second stage produces what looks like pink candyfloss where the leaf blades meet. These are the cotton-like strands of the mycelium, forming commonly when it is both warm and humid. As the infection spreads, small individual patches will join up to create larger pinkish-red areas.

What to look for

The first sign will be small, irregular-shaped patches of reddish-tinged grass. Look more closely and you will see evidence of one or possibly both stages of the disease, the tiny red needles and the pink mycelium.

Prevention is always best!

What causes it

Old gardening books talk about lack of nutrition as the main cause. Hence the treatment was to feed the lawn to encourage the diseased grass to grow out. We now know that weather plays an important role too, which explains why the disease can strike healthy as well as stressed turf.

Today's summer weather presents ideal conditions for red thread to flourish - hot, dry periods followed by cool, wet conditions, with dramatic changes in temperature (sometimes as much as 20 degrees within 24 hours).

How to treat it

As it attacks only the leaf parts, red thread is more of an aesthetic problem, although it can spread very quickly. However, feeding out (to speed up grass growth and then cut the affected grass) can remove the original blemish but at the same time spread the spores across a wider area (underfoot and via the mower). If you want to feed and cut, try mowing with a non-roller mower until the disease has improved as this will reduce the spread of the spores a little.

The only truly effective way to remove established red thread is with fungicides, and we do now have some safer modern chemicals derived from natural sources such as mushrooms. However, chemical treatments are still difficult to use correctly, and the best advice is to call in an expert to treat the grass safely and efficiently.

Prevention

My mantra for most lawn problems is to avoid them by maintaining a good lawn care programme! And this is true with red thread. In particular, keep thatch levels under control, remember to aerate your lawn, and try to keep the lawn surface as dry as you can.

Fusarium

Fusarium - also known as 'Snow Mould' - typically appears between September and March but you should keep an eye out for it throughout the year. Unlike red thread, fusarium can be fatal to the grass. Once it spreads from the leaf to the crown it will kill the plant - and this can happen very quickly!

What is fusarium?

Fusarium is a fungus that is widely found in the soil and on plants. The spores hibernate through the summer in the thatch and the soil. Then, when conditions are right (damp autumns and winter), dense white patches of fine, tiny cotton-like strands or fibres appear across the turf. The pathogen which actually kills the grass is *Microdochium nivale*.

What to look for

Fusarium is much more common on golf courses or finely mown lawns such as croquet lawns. If it does appear in your garden you will first see small orange patches, the size of a tennis ball, which can expand to the size of a dinner plate. Look closely and you will see the white mycelium on the surface like strands of candyfloss. You will typically see it when temperatures begin to drop in the autumn and grass growth slows down.

After 24-48 hours of the disease activating

A few weeks after first activating

What causes it

It is thought that fusarium particularly likes grass that is kept deliberately short. However it may simply be that this makes it easier to spot! Related conditions - too much thatch, soil compaction, dampness, lingering mists and still air - can all encourage the disease. A mild autumn and early winter can also be bad, as can applying too much nitrogen during this period.

How to treat it

Although rarer than red thread, fusarium can be devastating to the plants if not controlled as soon as possible. Just 48 hours can see your lawn become a dying mess so you need to act fast! A treatment with ferrous sulphate can help in the short term, as can keeping the grass as dry as possible in the autumn and winter. But to stop the pathogen from further affecting the plants, you need a chemical treatment, ideally applied by an expert as these are difficult to use correctly. Remember that whilst this prevents the pathogen from spreading further, any damaged grass may still require renovating or replacing.

Prevention

The same guidelines apply here as for red thread. Keep the thatch under control, the surface dry and remember to aerate the lawn. You can also ask an expert to apply a preventative chemical application in the early autumn.

The Runners-Up

Rust

Caused by the *puccinia* fungus, rust is a relatively common (although often unnoticed) disease but not one to worry too much about. The main problem is that once infected, spore-production can lead to it spreading quickly.

Spotting rust

Look out for a yellowing or orange appearance on the lawn (especially on coarser varieties of grass) in late summer. If it is quite bad you will also notice orange/yellow powder on your shoes or even on the mower.

Treating rust

Rust appears when the lawn gets very thirsty, so water deeply. An application of nitrogen can help, although you rarely need to consider any fungicide treatment for rust. Just remember to box off your clippings to avoid spreading the disease. If it gets out of control you may need to call in an expert to examine your lawn closely and give you advice.

Powdery Mildew

Powdery mildew, or *Erysiphe graminis,* is a fungus that creates a grey-white powdery growth on the upper surface of the leaf blade. Mildew prefers damp, low lit or shady areas and cool temperatures. The spores spread on the wind.

Spotting mildew

The first signs are little touches of the fine grey-white powder on the upper surface of the leaf. As the mildew increases it becomes denser, sometimes covering the entire leaf. In a really bad outbreak, whole areas of the lawn will be a dull white colour.

Treating mildew

You shouldn't get too worried by mildew, but if it is frequent in certain parts of the garden you can try to improve air circulation and/or prune back trees and shrubs to let more sunlight through. Do not try to treat mildew with a fungicide, and be careful when applying fertiliser as this can make the problem worse. Remember to box the clippings to prevent spread.

Others to Keep an Eye Out For

Much more rare are **Dollar Spot**, **Brown Patch** and **Slime Mould**.

Dollar Spot: a fungal disease which can kill the entire plant. Look out for silver-grey spots on the lawn from 2-14cm across

Brown Patch: a fungal disease with a characteristic appearance - circular brown patches from a few inches to several feet wide with greener grass in the middle

Slime Mould: unsightly but harmless spore-producing organisms which spread across the grass but often disintegrate on contact

Slime Mould

discussion.

Q: How can I avoid getting lawn diseases?

It's almost impossible to avoid them completely but you are not likely to suffer greatly from them either. As I keep repeating, good lawn maintenance is vital - a healthy lawn can actually fight off disease but a weak one will struggle.

Poor drainage and especially damp areas can encourage disease, so knowing how to maintain health in all parts of the lawn is important. Keeping the surface of the grass as dry as possible is useful and leaf blowers make less expensive alternatives to complex and probably unnecessary drainage systems. Try to get some light into shady and damp spots, and it helps to improve air flow too if you can. And remove leaves from the lawn as soon as they fall.

Also, be observant. Nowadays, diseases don't always follow the yearly timetables of out-of-date gardening books - they will appear whenever the conditions are suitable. At least if you spot a disease early you can take action to prevent it spreading.

Q: I've heard you can use moss killer to fight disease; is that true?

Yes - a treatment of ferrous sulphate (moss killer) can help during the winter by locking up the available nutrients (for example, left over from your autumn feed) whilst also drying out the leaf blade. It is not a cure, but it can help.

Q: What should I definitely NOT do?

Never feed too late in the autumn with food that contains a lot of nitrogen. Also, don't just leave it to nature to sort it out; if you have a disease in your lawn, you must follow good lawn hygiene. Ensure clippings are removed and boxed away from the lawn. And avoid mowing if you can as this will spread the spores.

*A stressed lawn
full of red thread*

Q: Are there non-chemical treatments I can use?

If you are lucky you may find something non-chemical which claims to work. But generally the best natural remedy is good lawn care. With the common diseases this often means getting better air circulation and/or light and also keeping the grass dry when you can. This will both prevent disease and reduce its spread if it does occur.

Q: What should I do with the clippings if I have a lawn disease?

It is perfectly safe to add these to your compost or put them in the garden recycling bin.

Q: My neighbour's lawn has a disease. Will my lawn catch it?

Some spores travel through the air and others can arrive via your footwear or even the paws of an animal, so yes, you might catch it from next door's garden. Try to remain vigilant and see if you can identify likely trouble-spots and improve the air and light conditions there.

pest control

Whilst weeds are undesirable but otherwise harmless, pests by definition do cause harm to plants. In lawn care, however, pests are mostly animals doing what nature intended but causing a few problems along the way. This is useful to remember as so much about good lawn care means working with rather than against nature. The casting earthworm, for example, does far more good aerating the soil than harm by leaving a few soil casts on the surface. So, before reaching for the exterminator, begin by assessing the problem. This short chapter explains how to do this, and suggests simple ways to manage or even prevent it.

"I am only going to talk about the most common pests; if you have something more exotic attacking your lawn you should seek specialist advice on any remedial action. In the UK we are very fortunate not to suffer the range of pest problems encountered, for example, in the US. However, the changing climate seems to be helping some pests to thrive more than before. Small populations are not necessarily harmful to your lawn - in fact, many pests go unnoticed for years. And in a poor-condition lawn it can be hard to distinguish between damage from pests and deterioration from neglect! As with most things lawn-related, the best control comes from being diligent, observing and monitoring on a routine basis".

Evidence of pests

Many pests remain invisible much of the time, staying underground and just leaving tell-tale signs on the lawn itself. It is useful therefore to know what evidence to look for, and which creature might be the culprit.

This bird might simply be pulling on a tasty worm - or it could also be foraging for plump chafer and leatherjacket grubs!

A sight that gardeners dread! The freshly tunnelled mounds of earth soon collapse down into the mole runs beneath, leaving behind a muddy mess on the surface.

Smaller than mole hills, these little granular mounds are tell-tale signs of busy ants below.

Birds will scratch around on the surface, but holes like these require strong paws, most likely those of a badger digging for grubs or a squirrel burying its winter food.

Our common pests

Crane Fly
(from the family *Tipulidae Sensu Stricto*)

The crane fly - which shares its informal name 'Daddy Long Legs' with the Harvestman - is our most common lawn pest that can do actual damage. Buzzing around like giant mosquitos, the adults are actually quite harmless. It is the larvae, known as leatherjackets and growing up to 5cm in length, which damage the lawn. The adult crane fly lays hundreds of eggs in the soil during autumn. Weeks later these hatch and the grubs live in the soil, feeding on grass roots, stems and sometimes even leaves until the winter and then again in the spring, before pupating and finally emerging as breeding adults.

Look for tell-tale signs of brown and dying grass in winter

How you know they are there

The obvious sign is the presence of adult flies in the autumn, flying low or nestling on the grass. Evidence in the turf itself can be hard to spot but look out for small patches of brown or dying grass around January. More disruption is actually caused by other animals digging them out as food, so be aware that by eliminating the grubs you may be removing a valuable protein source in the food chain.

Evidence of larger animals digging for grubs

How to get rid of them

1. **Chemical:** the chemicals designed specifically to kill crane fly larvae are only available to certified professionals.

2. **Physical**: scarifying and aerating will interrupt their feeding habits and so can be quite effective. Heavy rolling is not recommended; it *can* destroy the eggs but of course you need to know exactly *when* they are in egg form and to monitor the soil moisture carefully to prevent physical damage to the sward.

3. **Biological**: you can try using nematodes as a natural control. The pathogenic nematode *Steinernema feltiae* invades the grub and gives it a fatal fungal infection. Precise control however is not easy, with correct soil temperature and moisture levels critical to the success of the little worms.

Chafer Grubs

Chafer grubs are the larvae of chafer beetles, the two most common species in our lawns being the Garden Chafer (*Phyllopertha horticola*) and the Cockchafer (*Melolontha melolontha*). They live in the soil and eat the roots of the grass.

Garden Chafer: less common than the Cockchafer, this insect has a one-year lifecycle. New adult beetles breed and lay eggs around May or June and the larvae hatch shortly after and begin feeding immediately. By the autumn they are fully grown to approximately 15mm. They can continue to cause damage into the winter unless the cold forces them to dig down deeper in the soil. In spring they pupate and re-emerge in May/June as adult beetles.

Cockchafer: much more troublesome, this insect has a 3-4 year lifecycle, most of which is as a grub feeding greedily on your grass roots. The larvae grow up to 40mm in length. After pupation the new adults emerge at night making a sound like a bumble bee.

How you know they are there

With the destructive activity taking place beneath the surface it can be hard to know they are there. Look out for small brown patches of turf in the autumn, although the changing environment may impact on breeding patterns. You are much more likely to see damage caused by other animals (birds, badgers, moles, etc) as they dig in the lawn for the delicious fat grubs feeding just below the surface. If you suspect this and can lift parts of the lawn with your hands, you have a problem!

How to get rid of them

Treatment options are exactly the same as for crane fly larvae (see p178) - good regular maintenance (scarification and aeration) and, if necessary, the services of a qualified professional pest exterminator or lawn control company. As with the crane fly, heavy rolling is not recommended, and in any case will only destroy the new season's eggs, not the long-living larvae.

Worms

There are believed to be some 2700 types of earthworm in the world, around 29 of which are found in the UK - and only three of these cause any kind of problem, the casting worms. Even these, however, do more good than harm, burrowing through the soil to aerate it and ingesting organic matter before expelling it as usable nutrient. The problem is simply the soil casts they leave on the surface during wet or damp weather.

How to get rid of them

The worms are our friends, so it doesn't make sense to go on the offensive! If you do have an excessive problem, lawn specialists can use chemicals to discourage the worms from coming to the surface, or you can use acidifying fertilisers and sulphate of iron and good quality lawn sand to achieve the same effect. However, you may simply want to remove the soil casts - they can actually blunt the mower blades, and because they are so rich in bacteria they can aid weed germination too. The best method is to sweep them up using besom brooms or, on very fine lawns, to use switch poles or drag-mats.

Ants

Ants are amazing little creatures, fascinating to watch and, in the UK, generally not harmful to people (although if you or your children like walking across the grass barefoot you may disagree!). They also help to keep aphid numbers down. However, they do create mounds of soil and finely chewed debris, little ant hills which are unsightly in the middle of the lawn.

How to get rid of them

1. **Chemical:** there are well-known brand names for popular types of ant-killer, but my advice regarding *any* chemical is to seek help from a lawn or pest expert.

2. **Physical:** ant nests go down deep into the soil, so digging them up is unrealistic. Some people pour boiling water onto the nests but, again, it can be hard to penetrate all the way down and there is a risk of damaging the grass at the same time.

3. **Biological:** there is a safe and organic way to reduce your ant problem - apply used coffee granules to the areas they inhabit. Try it - it can work; just remember to flood with water afterwards! Nematodes (*Steinernema feltiae*) can and will remove them, but again are difficult to use as they need precisely the right environmental conditions. Finally, orange oil is sometimes thought to be effective as is Borax (also known as sodium borate, sodium tetraborate and disodium tetraborate) mixed with sugar. If you want to try these methods, place any of these in a container near the ant hills, not directly onto the grass.

Moles

Most people quite like this cuddly-looking little animal - we just don't like the big holes they dig in the lawn and the mounds of earth left behind! It's worth remembering, however, that when they do this they are only trying to eat, feeding on other pests such as chafer grubs, leatherjackets and worms. Fortunately for the mole, being larger and more akin to pet rodents than malicious-looking insects, more effort has been put into humane control methods.

How to get rid of them

1. **Chemical:** there are no chemical treatments available to the domestic user; you must hire a professional pest controller if you want to use this method (but please do look at humane control first).

2. **Physical:** the only physical intervention is to trap them, and there are humane and inhumane ways to do this. Trapping can actually be very effective but it takes time, and often people lose patience and resort to eradication. If you can try, however, trapping the little mole humanely and removing it to a different location where it can happily do what moles do has to be a good option.

3. **Biological:** there are no specially devised biological controls but a few homespun methods can work, thanks to the highly sensitive mole nose. First - the pickled egg down the mole hole; it's true! The smell from the egg, especially as it starts to rot, will force the moles to retreat. It does require perseverance (and many eggs) but you can be strategic in choosing the direction you want them to retreat in. Another option is to use human hair which they apparently do not like. Garlic has the same effect.

Larger pests

By definition, larger animals like squirrels, badgers and even deer are also pests. As with birds and moles, they are simply trying to feed, sometimes on the very pests you are already trying to get rid of. Control of this size of pest really can only be done by some form of physical barrier to prevent them from reaching the lawn. Or you might take a different view and enjoy observing these fine animals as they pay you the courtesy of a visit!

discussion

Q: I have birds pecking on my lawn. How do I get rid of them?

It is completely natural for birds to explore the lawn for food but it can be a nuisance once they find some rich pickings! So, a little investigation is necessary - identify which pest they're trying to excavate and then refer to the relevant section above to address the problem. You can also try techniques used in allotments and vegetable gardens - hanging reflective CDs, creating contraptions from plastic water bottles which rotate in the wind, etc. Just remember not to endanger the bird in any way.

Q: What can I do about the damage made by chafers in my lawn?

Whether it is the grubs eating the roots or the birds digging around for the grubs, the damage can be very irritating. It's best just to start again, removing the affected turf and soil and repairing with turf or seed containing the same grass mixture.

Q: What can I do about mole damage?

First you need to try to remove the mole. Other than this, all you can do is to repair the damage (reseed or returf) but remember to reuse the well-broken-down soil from the mole hill, either in the seed-bed or as a top dressing.

repairing problem areas

INCLUDES: Thin lawns and bare patches; shady areas; narrow walkways; when to reseed

Every lawn has its problems such as bare patches, poor grass growth, awkward places underneath shady trees or bumpy areas. These problems don't always arise from poor lawn care but can be from tough growing conditions or heavy usage that put additional stress on the lawn. They can always be improved or repaired to some extent; sometimes this will have to be an annual renovation job but often you can simply draw on the routine lawn care techniques in your 12-month programme.

We'll look at three typical problem areas - bare patches, shady areas and narrow walkways - and, because repair almost always involves some reseeding, we will also consider some strategies for this.

Thin lawns and bare patches

Swings and football goals, the turning point at the end of mowing rows, the six-foot stretch where the dog screeches to a halt - all these and more can leave you with very thin grass or even a completely bare patch. One option, of course, is to returf (see Turf and Returfing p116) but this can be expensive, especially if you have to do it each year. It may also upset the balance of grass types. A cheaper alternative involves some basic lawn care techniques and then reseeding.

1. Start by aerating the area - or if it needs it, why not do the whole lawn? If the lawn is really thin, you can aerate two or even three times.

2. Now you will have soil cores all over the surface of the lawn. Leave them there to dry out for an hour or so. Then, if you have a really bad area, use a broom or rake to transfer some cores here from the better parts of the lawn.

3. Preferably using a flail-bladed scarifier, make a pass over the problem area with the blade set just above the ground. This breaks up the cores, giving you a free seed bed!

4. Apply seed evenly by hand or using a drop-seeder.

5. Then go over the area with the scarifier again (blade still set above ground level) but this time at a different angle. This will break up more soil nice and evenly and cover much of the seed at the same time, creating the perfect environment for them to germinate.

6. Finally, wait for nature! The seeds should germinate and easily send down roots into the core holes.

Narrow walkways and paths

Many gardens, especially those that have been landscaped, have small and often narrow walkways between sections. These are vulnerable to a high or concentrated traffic rate, leading to excessive compaction of the soil. Shade and drought are also common problems thanks to the buildings or hedges and trees which commonly border the walkways. The result is that the grass roots are competing for water while its leaves are starved of sufficient sunlight. Throw in the tendency for these little areas to be the most neglected, and you can see why *regular* attention is so important. A quick-fix will only ever be short-lived; these are areas which really do need some extra nurturing.

General care

- Plan to renovate your walkways every year.

- Try to tackle the problem when there are optimum seeding and growing conditions, *not* just when it suits you. This may mean you have to cordon off the walkway at inconvenient times, but the results will be worth it.

- Be aware that these areas often fill out with annual grass varieties (especially annual meadow grass), giving a false impression that they are in better condition than they really are. Monitor the area throughout the year to gauge just how much the grass is struggling.

- Remember that much of the problem is *beneath* the surface in the compacted soil, and not necessarily in the mix of grass species.

Shady areas

The basic problem in a shady area, whether behind a wall or under a tree, is that the grass cannot photosynthesise adequately. Not surprisingly, therefore, the remedies mostly relate to light conditions and finding which grass varieties thrive better than others in this challenging situation. Each shady area is a unique micro-environment - some might only be shaded at certain times of the day while others may be permanently shady, and any nearby plants will compete vigorously for nutrients and water. So you need to look at the entire area objectively and decide how much you are able or willing to improve the conditions for the grass. Options include:

- Thinning out as much of the shade barrier as possible without harming the hedge, tree or plant

- Keeping leaves off the area during autumn/winter; the grass is already weak, and rotting leaves will add to the dampness and encourage disease or even kill off the grass in already-thinning areas

- Always cutting the grass at a higher to help it retain its strength.

Sometimes the best you can do is to incorporate an *annual* renovation and reseeding every spring. But of course, the best advice is to observe which grass species are thriving and use these when you reseed. For example, if you find that ryegrasses are thriving, don't automatically go for a 'shade' mixture; and if fescues are doing better, then a 'wear' mix may not be ideal for you.

When to reseed

This is the million dollar question when repairing badly worn and shady areas and, until quite recently, the answer would generally have been autumn. However, with the shifting climate there are now benefits to bringing this forward into the spring months (especially for shady areas) when:

- The trees will not be about to drop their leaves onto newly seeded areas

- The sunlight can still permeate overhanging trees

- The natural rainfall may be sufficient without you having to waste additional water (and time)

- The slowly rising temperatures that we now get will help this earlier germination.

By contrast, leaving it until autumn means regular leaf removal (which often leads to damage to the newly germinated seedlings), a greater risk of heavy (and colder) rainfall and even the possibility of soil temperatures dropping too fast for any germination at all. Apart from the leaf fall, the same benefits and disadvantages apply when reseeding worn areas of the lawn.

discussion

Q: What can I do to prevent soil compaction in my busy walkways?

Ideally you would widen the path to spread the load - but that is very rarely a realistic solution! So, what you *can* do is to help absorb the impact before it gets through to the soil. A good way is to use a product like 'crumb rubber' (basically shredded car tyres) to create a protective barrier between the surface and the soil. First aerate the soil well, then either create this new layer *or* mix the crumb rubber with your top dressing material before reseeding the area.

Q: When should I use sand as a dressing?

Beware - sand will rarely turn a wet lawn into a dry one! And there can be quality issues too as it is hard to be precise about different grades of sand. So when is it safe to use? The answer is only when you use with extreme care. It can solve little problems but cause big ones.

Dressing with sand will improve heavy or clay soils and help drainage, and it can dilute thatch levels too. Too much, however, can dry out the surface too much, exacerbating the problems. Sand is inert and not much help for seed germination, so if you do need to use a sand-only dressing, alternate it with a sand/soil mix.

Another warning - avoid sand with iron in it ('lawn sand') as it is prone to scorching the grass.

Avoid using builder's or sharp sand like this

Q: Which seed is best for shade and which is best for high-use areas?

Let's consider shade first. Yes, you can buy 'shady area seed' - but you won't always know if that is the reason for good results; it might also be because you thinned out the canopy above, or due to some other lawn care intervention. Also, what works well one year does not always work well every year. So, some species do appear to germinate successfully without much sunlight - fescues are notoriously good in shade - but as always, why not try out different species? You might be surprised by what works!

And for high-use areas? Well, the answer is almost the same - regardless of what it says on the packet, other considerations like soil protection (crumb rubber, aeration, etc) will play a part in the final outcome. And if you neglect these, even the best seed might struggle. So, it comes down again to good overall care and some patient trial and error.

additional problems
levelling

Levelling your lawn can range from a few minor repairs to a massive project. So, before committing yourself, think carefully about the final finish you want and the time you are prepared to put into your subsequent lawn maintenance. For example, is it really worth the effort of trying to create a bowling-green surface if you are not able to maintain it with an intensive care programme?

Below are just a few tips to help you.

A lawn covered in bumps

If you have a really uneven, bumpy lawn there are three ways to level it:

1. (the most arduous option) repair it bump by bump: using the technique for individual bumps, outlined below, rectify each bump and each dip until you achieve the evenness you want.

2. (the most expensive option) start from scratch: remove all turf, rotovate, relevel the ground and then seed or lay turf.

3. (the compromise option) simply spray off all living grass with glyphosate, add a new layer of soil and reseed.

However, do remember that in the years that follow you will need to manage your thatch and mowing techniques well in order to prevent new bumps and dips from appearing.

Individual hollows/dips

Here you need to open up the turf in order to fill in the dip with fresh soil. Start by marking out a square which comfortably exceeds the problem area. Then cut the turf diagonally corner to corner and, carefully lifting the central points of the turf, gently peel them back to expose the earth below. Then simply pack the hollow with soil to the desired height and replace the turf.

Individual bumps

This is much easier to rectify than a dip. Simply hollow-tine the area several times during the year. Gradually the mound will start to lower all by itself.

additional problems
fairy rings

Fairy rings - or elf circles, pixie circles and other such names - are intriguing and frustrating occurrences in our lawns. Unfortunately there is not very much that can be done about them but this short section will at least help you to understand what causes them and what to try if you really cannot tolerate them.

What are they?

Put very simply, fairy rings are the result of a soil fungus. Quite why they suddenly appear out of nowhere on a lawn is a mystery but experience shows that they often appear near to a tree - or close to where one once stood.

As the fungus becomes more prevalent it turns the soil hydrophobic, coating the soil particles and plant roots in a resin-like material which stops it from absorbing water. The effect is similar to a 'dry patch' in the soil where the soil particles struggle to retain moisture.

Variations

There are three common types of fairy ring:

1. A ring of well-growing grass with or without mushrooms (inspect the soil closely and you may see the beginnings of a white mycelium fungus coating it, with a characteristic musty smell)

2. A dark ring of greener grass with a ring inside this of dead grass where nothing will grow

3. Mushrooms at damp times of the year roughly forming a circular shape.

What can be done?

In the past there were chemicals which helped to remove the fungus but these have long since disappeared (and were only available in 'industrial' quantities unsuitable for domestic use). This leaves you with two options:

Soil replacement: dig out and replace the soil anywhere up to a metre in depth and half a metre beyond the circumference of the ring. Be warned, however - this is a lot of soil and may prove fruitless as there is no way of being sure that the mycelium are not active nearby.

Soil repair: here the aim is to reverse the fungal soil condition, a lengthy process requiring regular effort. Aerate the affected area to a depth of 4-10". Then use a watering can to apply wetting agents (or, for a cheap alternative, washing-up water) which over time will slowly reverse the fungal consequences by removing the resins from the soil particles. You then need to scarify the area and overseed until eventually grass starts to grow there. You need to do this procedure as often as you can throughout the year, continuing less regularly once the seed is germinating well.

Prevention

The only thing which may help prevent the fungus from taking hold is to keep your soil healthy with aeration and to keep the thatch under control with scarification.

additional problems

extreme weather

"My garden was submerged by flood water for a fortnight – what should I do?"

"We've had a kind of permafrost for nearly two months – will the lawn be dead?"

"My grass looks completely dead after weeks of drought."

Whatever your views about global warming, the 21st century has so far given us some alarmingly extreme weather. And lawns, often the largest and most visible areas of the garden, illustrate the impacts of this most clearly. Blankets of white snow, stretches of parched grass and cracking soil, and water, water, everywhere, from stubborn little pools which refuse to drain to huge lakes; the lawn is like the blank canvas on which nature paints vivid images of its startling power.

So, should we be worried, and what can we do about it?

First, let's remember two important facts. One, grass is one of the Earth's most resilient plants, and two, good lawn care is all about working with, not against, nature. However, I realise that these may not provide immediate comfort as you survey the damage after an autumn storm, or step outside day after day to monitor the flood waters in your garden. And if you have been putting in extra work to keep your lawn looking great, this experience can be truly soul-destroying.

The good news is that, given time, nature always rights itself after a blow. So, the first thing we need is to trust that it will and to be patient while it does. Of course, there are things we can do both to mitigate against future damage and to help our lawns recover just that little bit more quickly. And the part of the lawn structure that suffers the most is not the grass itself but the soil. Grasses can be reworked, thatch is rarely directly affected by the extreme weather incidents, but anything that upsets the important balance in the soil between solids, air and water will impact on the lawn.

Water

We face ever-increasing periods of hard and powerful rain. By itself this wouldn't be a huge problem if we didn't also have issues arising from land-management practices which appear to have upset the naturally evolved channels for water drainage (and remember, this happens in our own gardens too where we have replaced natural surfaces which filter rainfall with impermeable stone and concrete). And as we start to take an interest, we have all become much more familiar with the terms 'flood plain' and 'water table'. The effects of intense rainfall are becoming common problems for more and more of us, and seemingly at any time of year.

Let's say your lawn is saturated, perhaps having been flooded for a week or more. The important thing is not to leap in too soon; give the environment a chance to recover first. The water will eventually drain through and once it does, you don't need very many rain-free days, especially if there is a good wind, for the ground surface to become drier. Soon you will see healthy new grass shoots appearing, evidence that the lawn is alive and kicking.

The one thing you will need to do, eventually, is to aerate - and more regularly than you otherwise would. The excessive water will have squeezed the air out of the soil, leaving a compacted texture which roots cannot easily penetrate. First, however, you must allow time for the soil to drain a little - working on saturated soil will do more harm than good. In the meantime, you can also aerate if the water is still struggling to drain through - a simple hollow tine that penetrates the top few inches will help.

Another common problem is the small pool of water which collects and refuses to drain. This could, of course, have little to do with extreme rainfall and more to do with the substrate in that particular spot. You can try some hollow-tine aeration to improve the water percolation through the surface, but if it occurs because the water table has risen in recent years you may need to install drainage pipes. Before taking this drastic step, however, do be sure that the water can be efficiently removed and doesn't simply go straight back to the high water table.

Drought

In prolonged dry periods your lawn can take on the appearance of a dead wilderness - but the grass will revive. It's the soil that we need to worry about. Drought conditions lead to soil shrinkage, especially in the upper part of the profile. Although you will see cracks appearing, the air is actually being squeezed out of the surrounding soil. This is why aeration is so important, following your usual routine or doing it at the same time as any scarifying or overseeding.

What about watering? Well, to counter the effects of drought would take an immense quantity of water and time - much better for you and for the environment at large to leave this to nature. Eventually, natural rainfall will bring the soil moisture levels back to normal, and then you can implement any recovery work you have planned in the meantime.

Snow and frozen ground

When the ground is frozen, nothing happens - it's like putting food into the freezer, it goes into an inert state. The air and water in the soil will still be there. And if the lawn is then covered by a blanket of snow for any length of time, nothing especially bad will happen.

However, snow lying on top of non-frozen soil can be a problem. Don't be fooled by the chilly temperatures; the snow will act like a warm canopy over the ground, creating an ideal environment for disease pathogens to activate. So, once the snow has thawed, keep a vigilant eye out for signs of disease.

Wind

Powerful, gusty winds are an increasing occurrence and whilst they don't directly harm the lawn, broken branches and other debris certainly can. It is important to be vigilant and repair any damage to the lawn (don't just leave holes to be covered up by the surrounding grass). And try to remove debris manually - if you use the mower you will simply blunt or damage the blades.

And in general…

Don't panic - and remain patient. While the extreme weather persists, revise the chapters on routine maintenance. As soon as the weather returns to some kind of normality and the ground is recovering, you'll want to resume your lawn care programme, adding in any repairs that are needed.

12-month programme

Contents:

12-month programme

The essence of good lawn care is to develop a year-round programme that works for you and for your lawn. This means:

1) understanding what you're working with (the grasses, soil conditions, etc)
2) monitoring the impact of the weather, and
3) experimenting to discover what works and what doesn't.

It might take two or three annual cycles for you to establish the best programme for your lawn, and if the environmental conditions evolve, then so too will your programme.

The tables, charts and tips in this section will help you to develop just the right programme to maintain your lawn the way you want it.

Interventions at a glance

This simple chart shows the times of year that are suitable for each main intervention. For example, if you suddenly realise you haven't scarified for a whole year, this will help you decide when you might programme it in. With the exception of mowing, don't use this as a guide to the frequency of intervention, just the choice of months!

NB: for more information about what to do and when, use the Month-by-Month Planning section and of course for more detail, refer to the relevant chapter earlier in the book.

	JAN	FEB	MAR	APR	MAY	JUN	JULY	AUG	SEP	OCT	NOV	DEC
MOWING (per month)	1	1	2-4	4-6	4-8	4-8	4-8	4-8	4-6	2-4	2	2
FEEDING	✓	✓	✓	✓	✓	✓	✓	✓	✓	✓	✓	✓
WEEDING			✓	✓	✓	✓	✓	✓	✓	✓		
SCARIFYING			✓	✓	✓				✓	✓		
AERATION	✓	✓	✓	✓	✓				✓	✓	✓	✓
MOSS CONTROL	✓	✓	✓	✓	✓				✓	✓	✓	✓
SEEDING			✓	✓	✓	✓	✓	✓	✓	✓		
DISEASE CONTROL	✓	✓	✓	✓	✓	✓	✓	✓	✓	✓	✓	✓
TURFING	✓	✓	✓	✓	✓	✓	✓	✓	✓	✓	✓	✓
TOP DRESSING			✓	✓	✓	✓			✓	✓	✓	
CHAFER CONTROL	✓	✓	✓	✓	✓	✓	✓	✓	✓	✓	✓	✓
DADDY LONG LEGS	✓	✓								✓	✓	✓

Month-by-Month Planning
January & February

At this time of the year lawns and soils are cold and sometimes wet and the weather does not encourage gardening! However, some pests are still active, busily chomping away at your roots, and the changeable winter climate can create unexpected problems. Some diligence and a few hours of hard work now can make a big difference to the year ahead.

What	How & When
Thatch	Right at the beginning of the season is a good time to take a thatch measurement. This will give you advance warning of possible problems if it gets out of control further into the growing season.
Mowing	Try to give your lawn a light top-off once each month. This stops the lawn getting too leggy and will help the grass to dry out a bit better.
Aeration	If the weather is acceptable (moist but not too wet or frozen) this is a good time to hollow-tine aerate your lawn. For a small lawn, use a hollow-tine aerating fork and for a larger one use or hire a pedestrian machine. It is best to remove the cores from the surface. You could also do some very thin pencil tining and some slitting, but remember that this should be done more regularly and in conjunction with hollow-tine aeration.
Feeding	Try to find a good winter feed containing almost no nitrogen at all but with some element of phosphorous, potassium and iron. Alternatively, just apply a light-to-medium rate of iron (ferrous sulphate).

Disease	Diseases can appear very quickly over the winter when plants are under stress from cold, wet and windy weather. When you are out moving leaves off the lawn, keep an eye out for unsightly patches indicating disease.
Debris	Keep as much material off the lawn as possible. It seems a thankless task but lingering leaves do an enormous amount of harm to the lawn and encourage disease. Also brush off any worm casts that appear.
Repairs	There are two repairs you can do now: 1) if you have an uneven surface, this is a good time to do some levelling (p198) and 2) if you have any very poor grass patches, dig them out and replace with a new piece of turf.
Edges	There is no better time to straighten out those misshaped edges. Use your edging tool to give better definition to your lawn's perimeter.
Tools	January/February is a great time to make sure all your lawn tools are in great shape for the coming spring. The mower should be serviced, spare blades and edging tools need sharpening and all moveable parts should be oiled.
Frost	You will undoubtedly get some frosts during this month so remember to keep off the lawn whilst the frost is white. Walking can cause a burning appearance due to leaf damage which, although not always permanent, can be quite unsightly.

Month-by-Month Planning

March

March is when our minds start turning to the garden. We start sprucing up the shed, combing through old seed packets, cleaning pots - and thinking about the lawn. The trouble is that spring is very unpredictable. If the weather begins to improve, soil temperatures start to rise and the grass soon starts to grow. If it is a poor Spring, hardly anything seems to be happening. Being prepared to implement or to adapt your programme is really important.

What	How & When
Mowing	Be ready to get back into a mowing routine, but continue to mow at a sensible height, lowering it very gradually as you begin to mow more frequently.
Aeration	If the weather continues to be suitable this is another good month to hollow-tine aerate your lawn (see January for details). And continue to solid tine and slit, where required.
Scarification	As the ground temperature begins to rise, this is a great time to be scarifying, especially if you are doing a 'renovation scarification'. A good early scarification can give your lawn plenty of time to recover before summer arrives.
Feeding	If feeding in March isn't in your programme but you are scarifying your lawn, apply a good balanced feed afterwards. This will allow the new grasses to flourish once all that moss and debris have gone.
Moss	If you are doing a renovation or maintenance scarification, now is a perfect opportunity to apply a moss treatment. Remember to do this after scarification, not before, so that the moss killer can kill the moss plants and spores at the base of the sward.

Disease	Continue to be vigilant with diseases - with changing weather patterns, disease patterns are also changing.
Debris	Keep material off your lawn (although you should be free by now of the last of autumn's leaves).
Repairs	Now is still a good time to start or continue those minor repairs (see January).
Seeding	If the temperature is rising, you can begin sowing seed to take advantage of some early spring sunshine.
Top dressing	Growth should be picking up now, so if you have plans to apply any dressing material, between now and June now is your chance.
Weeds	As it gets warmer, weeds can begin to germinate. You can start applying selective herbicides if you want to use them.

Month-by-Month Planning
April

April is often when you can start to enjoy the rewards of your early work. The temperature is rising, the grass is growing and enjoying regular cuts; spring fertilisers will be kicking in and, if you were able to scarify and aerate during March, the sward will be filling in nicely.

What	How & When
Mowing	Continue to mow at a sensible height, slowly lowering the height as you increase regularity. If using a rotary mower, your aim is gradually to reach the optimum no lower than 25mm.
Aeration	If the weather is still suitable (not too wet or dry) you still have time to hollow-tine aerate the lawn with an aerating fork or a pedestrian machine. By April, however, you need to be careful about slitting as there is a risk of the slits staying open and the lawn drying out.
Scarification	As with March, April is still a great time to be scarifying, especially if you are doing a 'maintenance scarification'.
Feeding	If feeding in April isn't in your programme but you are scarifying your lawn, apply a good balanced feed afterwards. This will allow the new grasses to flourish once all that moss and debris have gone.

What	How & When
Moss control	If you are doing a renovation or maintenance scarification, now is a perfect opportunity to apply a moss treatment. Remember to do this after scarification, not before, so that the moss killer can kill the moss plants and spores at the base of the sward.
Debris	Keep material off your lawn, especially prior to any mowing.
Repairs	It's not too late! (see January)
Seeding	Late spring temperatures and sunshine are great for seed germination.
Top dressing	May and June are the last months suitable for heavy top dressing before summer beds in (unless you have an irrigation system).
Weeds	Weeds will be enjoying the warming temperatures and sunshine, so you can apply selective herbicides if you wish (unless it is an unusually dry early summer).

Month-by-Month Planning

May

Early scarified lawns should now have recovered, grass growth should be at its optimum rate, flowers are beginning to pop up - and the late spring/early summer garden swings into life.

What	How & When
Mowing	Maintain your mowing schedule, lowering the height very slowly as you mow more often (but keep to the guiding rule of not cutting more than one third of the existing leaf).
Aeration	Aeration dries out the surface, so be very careful going into these months. Hollow-tine aeration can be done but be prepared to water if the weather turns dry, and avoid slitting.
Scarification	As with aeration, a dry spring can make it unsuitable to scarify during May. If you need to scarify, make it a very light one.
Feeding	If your own programme includes a May feed, try to avoid using feed with a high iron content and lawn sands as these products can scorch the grass when conditions are dry.
Moss	If you have to scarify, then you can follow through with moss killer but keep it very light to avoid scorching. If the weather is dry, use a liquid application. Dead or dying moss does not have to be jet black! Read the instructions carefully and use high water volume to reduce the scorch risk.

Repairs	You can continue with minor repairs including seeding.
Debris	Keep the lawn free of debris, and if you have trampolines, hammocks and garden toys, keep moving them around to different parts of the lawn.
Top dressing	May and June are the last months suitable for top dressing before summer beds in (unless you have an irrigation system).
Weeds	Weeds will be enjoying the warming temperatures and sunshine, so you can apply selective herbicides if you wish (unless it is an unusually dry early summer).

Month-by-Month Planning

June

Traditionally June has been a month of baked soils and parched brownness. More recently it has sometimes been a month of prolonged rainfall and cooler conditions. This can bring on diseases much earlier than we have grown to expect in the past. Weeds will also be celebrating any bonus moisture. But we should still be able to enjoy the beginnings of summer and the fruits of our hard work in preparing the garden for this moment.

What	How & When
Mowing	By now you will be into your comfortable mowing routine, enjoying the regularity and quality of the cut (but not too short - it's not Centre Court at Wimbledon!).
Feeding	You can feed in June but take the same precautions as for May to prevent scorching.
Debris	As always, keep the lawn clear of lingering debris and rotate any seasonal furniture and fittings (swings etc) if possible to avoid stressing the grass.
Repairs	If you have any repairs still to make, now can be your last chance. Be ready to water more than normal if conditions are dry.
Seeding	A good month for sowing as grass seed will love the warmth and sunshine of June.
Top Dressing	Unless you have an irrigation system, June is the last chance for light top dressing while growth is still strong.
Weeds	Weeds will be enjoying the warming temperatures and sunshine, so you can apply selective herbicides if you wish (but not during dry periods, especially with 'feed and weed' products).

Month-by-Month Planning

July/August

At last you can relax a little and really enjoy your lawn. The focus is on protecting it - raise the mowing height a little if it starts to get warm and dry. But remember, if it goes brown, it will eventually turn green again!

What	How & When
Mowing	As in June, maintain the regularity, take care with the quality of the cut, and be ready to raise the height a little to avoid stressing the grass. You can also return the clippings to the lawn to enhance food and water provision.
Feeding	You can feed in July, but to avoid scorching be careful not to apply products that have too much iron (FE). Liquids can be used for faster absorption and also to further reduce scorching risk.
Debris	The same rules still apply - remove debris and keep moving any summer fittings and furniture around to different parts of the lawn.
Weeds	Weeds don't take a summer holiday, so remain vigilant but be cautious about using any weed killer during hot periods.

Month-by-Month Planning
September/October

As autumn beds in, leading slowly towards the winter, there is still much pleasure to be had from the garden. The morning dew is a sign of cooling temperatures but be on the look-out for disease. However, this is mainly a time to be preparing your lawn for the winter with a little renovation work if you didn't do any in spring.

What	How & When
Mowing	Growth should be starting to slow down so you can begin reducing the regularity and at the same time gradually increase the cutting height.
Aeration	If conditions are moist enough you can consider an early aeration, but beware Indian summers when the lawn can easily dry out.
Scarification	This is a good time to start scarifying, whether for maintenance or moss control. If the moss is heavy, the earlier you start the better.
Feeding	If you are scarifying your lawn, apply a good, balanced autumn feed afterwards. With all the debris and moss gone, the new grasses can flourish. You can in any case apply a September feed if it is in your schedule.
Moss control	Whether you are doing a renovation or maintenance scarification, now is a perfect opportunity to apply a moss treatment. Remember to do this following scarification, not before, so that the moss killer can kill the moss plants and spores at the base of the sward.

Disease	Continue to be vigilant with diseases; our changing weather patterns mean that some diseases continue to hang around for longer.
Debris	Think about putting away summer furniture etc if you can. If not, continue to move it around the lawn periodically rather than leave it in one place all winter. Keep an eye out for falling leaves and remove these regularly.
Repairs	Now that the lawn is being used less frequently this is a good time to get round to any repairs you may have been putting off.
Seeding	With the dropping temperatures, you might consider reseeding now or leave it until the spring. It is often still warm enough, but germination may not be as reliable as you move towards the end of October.
Top dressing	The grass should still be growing so there is still time to apply a top dressing, if required.
Weeds	As the temperature drops and weeds recede, you are losing the chance to kill them until next year. Be sure to use the correct herbicide for any last attacks before the winter.

Month-by-Month Planning
November/December

Dropping temperatures and harsher diseases are a reminder to tidy up before winter really hits. Some diligence and hard work now will leave it in a healthy state and save you a lot of bother next year. Above all, keep an eye out - see what's happening; even if you can't do much about it (for example, sustained heavy rain) you can be preparing for remedial work in the spring.

What	How & When
Mowing	Continue to wind down your cutting programme, raising the cutting height as growth slows, but remember to keep the blades sharp to avoid stressing the grass by tearing it.
Aeration	If the weather is suitable, you can hollow-tine aerate your lawn. If you have a small lawn, use your hollow-tine aerating fork, or for a larger lawn, hire a pedestrian machine. Remember to remove cores from the surface. If you wish, some very thin pencil tining and some slitting are advisable - but remember that this has to be done more regularly.
Debris	As well as avoiding any area being covered by standing objects all winter, the other reason to keep the lawn clear now is to make sure the air can circulate and help the grass to dry off between rains.
Repairs	If you still haven't got round to any little repairs it's not too late! See January for some inspiration.

Two easy-starter programmes

If you are completely new to the idea of a maintenance programme, you might find one of these simple programmes helpful - one is for a utility/everyday lawn and the other for a luxury lawn. You can use these as your starting point and then, by observing what happens - what works well and what doesn't - and making notes, you can adapt this programme year by year. You will soon become an expert on your own lawn!

Utility Lawn

Jan-March	Hollow-tine aerate (remove cores from the surface)
March	Scarification Light maintenance or renovation type
March	Moss treatment A liquid application works best
March	Spring feed and weed treatment Apply weed killer separately, if possible
June	Summer feed and weed treatment Apply weed killer separately, if possible
September	Autumn feed and weed treatment (more-resistant weeds) Apply weed killer separately, if possible
December	Winter feed treatment A low nitrogen (2-4%) feed, with iron and potassium

Luxury Lawn

(this is just an example to get you started but any luxury lawn will require a very carefully planned programme based on actual experience with your lawn)

Jan	Hollow-tine aerate (remove cores from the surface)
March	Scarification A maintenance scarification only
March	Moss control A liquid application works best
March	Top dressing application (sand/soil) Use a 70/30 type mixture
March	Spring feed and weed treatment Apply weed killer separately if possible
June	Summer feed and weed treatment Apply weed killer separately if possible
June	Preventative 'red thread' treatment Use a fungicide spray *
June	Top-dressing application (sand/soil) Another light application, using a 70/30 type mix
September	Scarification A maintenance scarification only
September	Top-dressing application (sand/soil) Another light application, using a 70/30 type mix
September	Autumn feed and weed treatment Apply weed killers separately, if possible
October	Hollow-tine aerate Remove cores from surface
December	Winter feed treatment A low nitrogen (2-4%) feed, with iron and potassium

* Consider calling in an outside contractor for this.

NB - this programme does not include optional treatments such as wetting agents, colourants, insecticides, growth regulators etc.

Tips for keeping your own lawn care records

First, you have made a great start by getting this book. I hope it will provide stimulation and solutions to all kinds of problems for many years to come. However, I do hope you will feel motivated to follow through and create your own record of your lawn and its maintenance. This is particularly useful if you are planning to undertake any major change - whether an improvement project or large-scale redesign in the garden - and similarly if you experience any extreme weather event which throws your routine maintenance off course.

Become a detective! Most observations that you record may not, by themselves, mean very much. But once you start to look into a problem you encountered and start pulling together pieces of evidence, you can work out what caused what, and how to prevent it in the future.

WEATHER: if you want to keep good records it makes sense to monitor and record the weather, month by month - rainfall, average temperatures, frost and snow, etc - especially if you are monitoring different interventions year on year.

GRASSES: monitor the leaf blades each month for any discolouration or other signs of stress (eg from an excess of thatch suggesting a need to scarify more often).

THATCH: check the thatch every three months. You're looking for an increase in thatch production, especially after prolonged wet or dry periods.

SOILS: keeping notes on the soil can be a strong incentive to stick to your aerating schedule! A few months after aerating, check that you have strong new root development. You may also be tempted to keep records of pH measurements, but any change is likely to be so slight and of little practical use that this is not worth doing.

NUTRITION: you want to make the most efficient use of fertiliser, so capture all the obvious information - application dates and rates, product details, how quickly you first saw a positive response, how long before the efficacy began to weaken - as well as application information (problems with the spreader, the weather conditions etc).

WATERING: if you water your lawn, it's really important to avoid waste. It is therefore very helpful to monitor both the temperature and wind conditions (and water quantities if you can) when you water, and the results you achieve.

DISEASE: in addition to keeping a vigilant eye out for disease, make a note of when it first appears, the general conditions at the time, what action you took and how quickly the problem was cured.

PESTS: it can be useful to make notes about when daddy long legs typically appear in your lawn. Remember also to observe birds and other animals digging around in the turf.

WEEDS: you can record which weeds appear when, but the most useful information will be about any action you took, what you used, how you used it and what you achieved.

MOSS: it can be useful to record when moss occurs, particularly in relation to your thatch management programme.

appendices

all about
mowers

INCLUDES: Cylinder vs rotary; mower maintenance; discussion

Types of mower - cylinder vs rotary

Thanks to mower manufacturers, buying a mower can be both exciting and daunting. Designed to meet all needs, they range from the neat and lightweight to the stylish and muscular, and some even sport familiar names from the car world. And you can even buy rechargeable cordless mowers, ideal for eliminating the risks of cutting through the cable. So how do you choose? What is the right mower for you and for your lawn?

In essence, it's quite a simple choice - there are cylinder mowers and there are rotary mowers. Both types range from small, manoeuvrable devices to large sit-on machines, and both types come in petrol and electric versions. The difference is in the finish that each type delivers.

The cylinder mower

Cylinder mowers are used for the highest quality of finish on a lawn - you will see them in use, creating beautiful parallel stripes on tennis courts and in university quadrangles. Today's cylinder mower is not much changed from the very first mechanical mowers (see A Brief History of the Lawn, p16) and typically has a heavy roller at the back to create the striped effect, and a smaller roller at the front.

It gets its name from the cylindrical arrangement of the cutting blades which rotate very fast against a fixed strip of metal (known as the bottom blade). This scissor action results is a very tidy and sharp cut. The cutting and the bottom blades do not need to touch when regularly sharpened or adjusted, although too large a gap will lead to torn rather than cut blades of grass, damaging the plants.

The rotary mower

Designed in the 1930s, the rotary mower was developed for the growing domestic market. Cheaper to make than a cylinder mower, the rotary has a single blade rotating at high speed on a horizontal plane. The blade does not need close or actual contact with anything else, just the grass.

Arguably, the rotary method of cutting is not as good for the plants. While the cylinder mower uses a scissor action, the rotary cuts more like a scythe. With only a single blade, the process relies on the speed of its rotation and, of course, its sharpness, something often overlooked! In fact, for the most consistent results the blade should be given a quick sharpen every time you cut (see below for how to do this). Blunt blades tear the grass rather than cutting it, stunting the growth which leads to colour loss and inhibits food and water uptake.

Cylinder vs rotary: differences in use

The only significant difference in use between cylinder and rotary machines relates to the cutting height. You cannot expect to achieve the incredibly fine and short cut of a golf green using a rotary mower - so don't try! Simply use the golden rule of never cutting more than a third of the current height, and monitor the results - keep notes of the height setting you used and the result you achieved. Every lawn is different with different species growing at different rates.

However, each mower type does have its own characteristics:

A cylinder mower:	A rotary mower:
prefers to cut shorter grass	tends to scalp short grass
means more frequent mowing	can be used less frequently
uses much sharper blades	cannot cut as sharply as a cylinder
requires a much flatter surface	can cope better with more uneven surfaces
requires a stricter maintenance programme	requires less maintenance work
prefers a fine mixture with shorter length	can maintain most types of lawn

Mower maintenance - regular checks and cleaning

We tend only to think about mower maintenance in winter when we send it off for a service. However, it is a good idea to do some routine basic maintenance on a more regular basis. The tips below relate to both cylinder and rotary mowers except for blade sharpening. If you use a cylinder mower, this must be done by a professional.

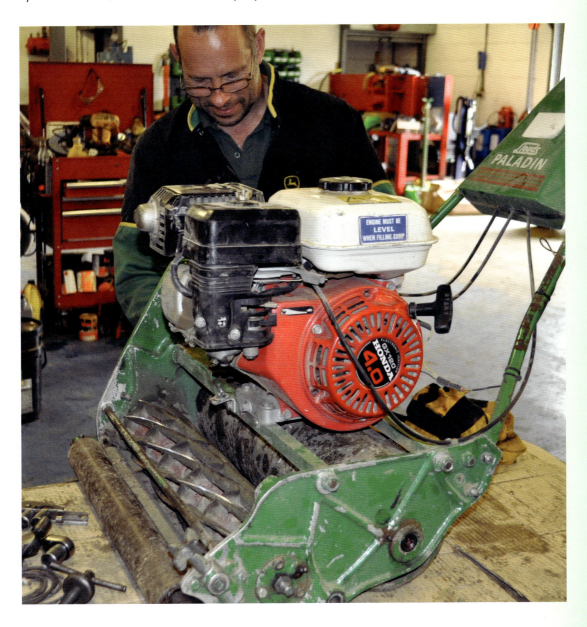

Pre-mowing checks:
Petrol mowers

1. Check fuel and oil levels; top up as required.

2. Check spark plug; clean if necessary with a wire brush.

3. Inspect your oil filter

4. Check your mower blade is sharp (for cylinder mowers, consult a professional)

5. Check your lawn mower height - it may have loosened and need readjusting to show a true reading.

6. If necessary, lubricate moving parts, wheels, etc with lubricating fluid (eg WD 40).

Electric mowers

Follow all the relevant steps from p232-233 AND examine cabling for any damage (with the power supply disconnected first).

And some others...

Ride-on mowers: usually resembling miniature tractors, most of these are rotary mowers and cut the grass in exactly the same way.

Mulching mowers: these use air-flow to chop the cuttings again inside the machine before casting them out as mulch.

After mowing:

1. Clean the underneath of the mower - use a brush, scraper, hose or pressure washer to clean well. The under-side of your mower is designed to create maximum airflow so any material sticking to the sides will stop grass being thrown into the box successfully (remember with electric mowers to disconnect the power supply first) and tip on its side so that the air filter is facing upwards.

2. Start the motor after cleaning to ensure smooth running.

3. Top up fuel ready for next time.

4. Check any moving parts for loose bolts etc.

5. Lubricate any bolts to prevent them seizing up.

6. Change over the spare blade where necessary.

7. Clean the grass-collector and allow it to dry.

discussion

Q: How often should I sharpen my blade?

This is a good question as blunt blades account for many of our least-attractive lawns!

If you use a cylinder mower, the blade must be sharpened by a specialist at least once a year. However, you should check every time you mow that the bottom blade is making contact with the cylinder and adjust it if necessary. You can also do the 'paper test' to check the blade cleanly cuts a sheet of paper. Tip the mower backwards. Then, carefully turning the blades, feed in a sheet of paper between the cylinder and the bottom blade. A sharp blade will give a clean cut but a blunt one will usually jam the paper just like a faulty printer does.

A rotary blade can need sharpening more often as it is the sharpness and speed which make the cut (not the scissor action of the cylinder mower). Most gardeners only have the blade sharpened once a year (if that) but in fact you should be sharpening it every 2-4 weeks from March onwards to avoid tearing and damaging the grass. You can do this using a file or even an angle grinder.

Sharpening a rotary blade.

Q: How can I set the cutting height?

With a cylinder mower it is possible to set the height very accurately. Most will require a set of simple tools - a metal bar, adjusting screws and so on which are usually supplied with the mower and are used to adjust the height of the rollers with great precision. Some cylinder mowers now have the cutting mechanism designed as a removable cartridge, making any adjustment work even easier, and others come with a selection of pre-set height - you just turn the dial.

It is not so easy to be precise with a rotary mower. The lawn is often cut higher than when using a cylinder mower, but because the mower sinks into the thatch it cuts lower than you realise. The best way to measure the height is to place the mower on a clear, flat surface and then try to measure the distance between the blade and the surface.

Q: My mower has several pre-set height settings. Which should I use?

Every mower is different - and so is every lawn. Not helpful, I know, but you need to get to know your mower and follow the steps above to establish the actual cutting heights. One tip, however, is not to use the two or three lowest settings on a rotary mower as this will probably damage the turf.

Q: Why does my lawn mower drop clumps of clippings when it's wet?

This can be because the underside of your mower is clogged with grass. Mowers are designed to generate maximum air and grass flow, but they need your help to maintain this, particularly if the grass is wet and sticky. Remember, however, never to put your hands near the blade when the motor is running.

Q: How can I make my stripes stand out even more?

Stripes can look fantastic if you have a special outdoor event planned! And it's easy to give them more definition. Either double cut on the day over the same lines, or try applying a seaweed and iron product a week or two before the event.

Q: Can I use a robotic mower?

Absolutely. In fact, since mowing regularly and with enough accuracy to ensure you take off no more than one third of the leaf blade is important, if you have a nice even lawn and can set the robot's computer with precision, why not? You won't get stripes but you'll be maintaining a cleanly cut lawn.

alternatives to grass

Anyone investing in this book is likely to prefer grass lawns to any alternative. I certainly do. However, there is definitely some justification for considering alternatives – and the reasons range from purely practical to the aesthetic. Here I briefly consider two – the chamomile/flower lawn and the artificial lawn – looking at both the strengths and drawbacks of these options.

Chamomile and flower lawns

If you read the short history of lawn care at the start of the book, you will know that in the early days anything vaguely resembling a cultivated lawn consisted of grass and flower meadows, kept shortened by grazing animals. More recently, with the vogue for landscape design and show gardens, there has been much interest in a lawn alternative which boast the colourful and fragrant benefits of flowers. To some these will never be lawns, but as a chiefly green area of the garden, completely concealing the soil below, they serve some of the same function. They have a few advantages too:

They need mowing or cutting only a few times a year (not the twenty or so cuts a grass lawn requires).

They don't demand regular chemical feeds - *but don't be fooled into thinking that modern lawn care is all chemical either! As I have said elsewhere, far fewer chemicals are used on the average lawn than in the rest of the garden.*

The flowers and variety of plants attract a greater number of bees and insects than grass alone.

Alternatives like the chamomile lawn can work really well in small and awkward spaces. Ultimately, however, it must be a personal choice. Some will only accept grass while others are very happy to sacrifice grass in favour of the delights of a flower meadow. Of course there is always a third way - a grass lawn with small patches of 'flower lawn' nearby!